ON
TOP
AGAIN

MICHAEL SHINER

ASPECT DESIGN
Malvern, Worcs. UK

Published by Aspect Design 2008
Malvern, Worcs. UK

Designed and Printed by Aspect Design
89 Newtown Road, Malvern, Worcs. WR14 1AN
United Kingdom
Tel: 01684 561567
E-mail: books@aspect-design.net
www.aspect-design.net

All Rights Reserved.
Copyright © 2008 Michael Shiner
All photographs reproduced in this book are copyright © 2008 Michael Shiner

The right of Michael Shiner to be identified as the author of this work has been asserted
in accordance with Section 77 of the Copyright, Designs and Patents Act 1988.

This book is sold subject to the condition that it shall not, by way of trade or otherwise,
be lent, resold, hired out or otherwise circulated without the publisher's prior consent in
any form of binding or cover other than that in which it is published and without a similar
condition including this condition being imposed on the subsequent purchaser.

ISBN 978-1-905795-20-8

ON TOP AGAIN

To the memory of Fiona, an early rejected
Golden Retriever from the RNIB
who proved herself a wonderful, obedient and
understanding companion in all that follows …
17th July 1984 – 9th November 1999

On Top Again

Part II

Part III

Preface

In writing of these adventures over the years I have to thank the Shepherds and Farmers of Mid-Wales and the Border Counties for their support and permission to walk upon their land; for their understanding and welcome for both of us.

I must also thank The Royal National Institute for the Blind for breeding, early training and eventually allowing me to purchase such a truly wonderful dog and as loyal a companion as one could ever have.

My gratitude also goes to the Staff of Aspect Design for guiding me into publication and correcting my errors along the way!

Any errors are mine and I accept that whatever others may find in directions and suchlike will undoubtedly have altered over the years in between; but one thing to be remembered is that the natural beauty of the Countryside will still be there together with its wonderful flora and fauna if one's eyes are open enough to see it: *enjoy.*

List of Helpful Welsh Phrases

Out on the hills and mountains of Wales
some of the following words and phrases may help.

English–Welsh

Good Morning .... *Bore Da*

Good Evening .... *Noswaith Da*

Good Night .... *Nos Da*

Thanks .... *Diolch*

Good .... *Da*

Very Good .... *Da Iawn*

How are you? .... *Sut Mae?*

Good Day .... *Dydd Da*

Thank you very much ...... *Diolch yn fawr Iawn*

Welsh–English

Aber .... *River Mouth*

Afon .... *River*

Glyn .... *Glen*

Llyn .... *Lake*

Bryn .... *Hill*

Maen .... *Stone*

Welsh–English

Bwlch .... Pass

Carreg .... Rock

Mawr/Fawr .... Great/Big

Cefn .... Ridge

Moel/Foel .... Bare Hill

Pant .... Hollow/Valley

Coch .... Red

Craig .... Rock

Pentre .... Homestead/Village

Crib .... Summit

Cwm .... Valley

Plas .... Mansion or Hall

Pont .... Bridge

Sarn .... Old Road

Dinas .... Fort or City

Uchaf .... Upper

Eglwys .... Church

Ystrad .... Valley Bottom

Croeso i Cymru .... Welcome to Wales

Introduction

Just over 20 years ago we started upon a little personal adventure that was to end in 1967 with 76 hill or mountain tops being climbed in Wales, all on expedition from Worcester on one's 'day off'. Now that retirement has become one's permanent 'day off', cautious selection of any day that meets up with reasonable weather offered the challenge to do some of those 76 peaks again! We started on February 4th 1987 and although the exact original order of climbing cannot be carried out now, nevertheless we started where it originally began, just outside Abergavenny. The only difference on this second time round, apart from being 20 years older myself, is that in order to have us on top again my companion has changed; that first series of expeditions I was accompanied by Marcus – a Black Labrador; this time it is Fiona – a Golden Retriever; she, like her predecessor, insists upon being photographed by the Trig. point, on top!

PART I

*Twelve walks or climbs of various degrees of difficulty,
to be found at around an hours drive from Malvern:
mostly over the Welsh border or in the Border counties alongside.*

BLORENGE
(1,833 ft.)

February 5th, 1987

Recorded as 552m on the Ordnance Survey map – Landranger 161 – we accepted the challenge in weather of poor visibility, fine though certainly not cold, on Wednesday, February 4th 1987. We left home at 08.15hrs and took the Ledbury–Ross–Monmouth road which got us to Abergavenny at 9.30am after some 45 miles. Out of the Town on the B4246 and heading for Blaenavon we left it just above Govilon where we turned left to find the 'Foxhunter Car Park' on Cefn-y-Galchen. Not then too far to walk on the first trip of the new series! Last time we did it from the cattle-grid much lower down on the main road but there was a quarry there then in which one could leave the car. The weather had slowly deteriorated into a mist with visibility some 600 yards; we 'booted and spured' and taking a map bearing, for safety's sake, we set off for the Trig. point on top. It took us a very leisurely hour to do the round trip but we did spend time on top remembering last time! Then it was snowing and in what turned out to be almost a 'white-out' situation suddenly, we had to re-trace our tracks down to the quarry in cautious haste. Now it was fog! The mist had thickened whilst we were on top photographing and drinking coffee so it was with great relief that the return bearing was already established and we had brought the trusty 'Silva' compass – the same one as that used 20 years ago. Safely back in the car park we both declared that it had been fun and sought the valley streamside for lunch before contemplating the return drive. Compared with 20 years ago what had changed? Nothing, really. Not from the walking point of view – it was still as beautiful, as quiet and as gauntly haunting on the top as it ever was. We had seen lambs in the fields and there was much snow lying under the hedges still – one a promise of spring and the other 'waiting for more', maybe? A day of undemanding exercise and a promising start to the new series of *On Top Again* adventures. The drive home along the main road through Hereford offered effortless driving but does not match up to the awe-inspiring little back road to our car park starting point! To find that you must look carefully into OS Map 161 and then get to Llanfoist (just outside Abergavenny) and start the climb from 292126! We both hope that you are a good and adventurous driver!

On the top of Blorenge (before the mist).

Off the narrow road from Llanfoist we found donkeys.

WHIMBLE
(1,965 ft.)

February 11th, 1987

This is a lovely place to find and in the opposite direction to last week's hill. On Ordnance map 148 we found our way from Malvern (where we live) on to the Hereford road (A4103) and turned off to Bromyard; thence to Leominster and onto the A44, signposted to Rhayader. After Kington (*not* to be confused with Knighton!) one comes to a little village called New Radnor and on this last stretch of main road there opens up before one the fine, majestic view of the surrounding hills and in many places their complement of conifer plantations – this area is still called Radnor Forest, reaching up to 2,166 feet on Great Rhos which today, sadly, is inside the military firing ranges that cover some of this wonderful part of Wales. It was for this reason that we selected Whimble as our second climb because in 1965 it was Great Rhos, now marked on the map as 'Danger Area' and we heard the firing across the valley.

Once into New Radnor you have to find a little, very steep lane at the back of the village which is enchantingly named 'Mutton Dingle'. Driving up this hill one has to hope that no tractor is coming down! At the top and the far end it enters Forestry Commission land and one can park there – we did, in a light drizzle! We had taken just over the hour to get there and some 45 miles of uncluttered roads going over the border into Powys just beyond Kington. As my canine companion explored the forest floor I changed into walking clothing; checked the pack and checked the map. A good track leaves this point to go round the forest on its western side and takes one to the bottom of Whimble – a lovely walk which was made the more exciting by the sighting of a buzzard, hunting low over the heather. As the track reaches higher ground and opens out there is a glorious view of the valley below and beyond, down which a stream runs from Harley Dingle above and out of sight. One can walk on into this area for a while and the silence is broken only by distant firing and the occasional roar of a low-flying jet. The sheep have it to themselves usually but today we shared their high and heather-clad domain.

Whimble lies above one here at a modest height to some but a demanding climb for others. It is almost straight up from the fence and very steep – not for the unwary. Our day was made for one of us at this point – Fiona (that is my Golden Retriever), was completely absorbed in her surroundings! As I looked up at Whimble it was snow covered for the last 200 feet and made breath-takingly beautiful in the now gentle sunshine. Over the fence and up the track that leads to the cairn on top. It was 11·00am exactly and we had left home at 8·00am – not bad for a not very promising February day and here we were in another world seemingly; above the traffic of the A44 trunk road winding its way to Aberystwyth; alone in the buzzard's territory with only occasional sheep for company. We sat and drank it all in and Fiona posed by the cairn for the photograph!

It is possible to make a detour on the return route to suit one's walking abilities; there is a track leading from the bottom of Whimble, just over the fence and it goes on up the valley and then either to Bache

Hill or further to Black Mixen at 2,002 and 2,135 feet respectively. We agreed that on another day, preferably when it was fine, dry and sunny, we would return to this beautiful valley but for the moment we retraced our steps and went down to the car. Taking our leave of the steep descent of Mutton Dingle we took the A44 as far as Lyonshall and then cross-country to Hereford and back home along the A438 reaching home in Malvern during the afternoon where, we learned, it had been raining hard, all day! 'On Top' for the third time next week, ought to see us back outside Abergavenny where a 'sweet hill' of some 1,955 feet awaits us – perhaps our prayer for that ought to be 'Give us this day our daily bread'? See you there, next week.

NB. If you have the time after climbing Whimble why not take the car up the A44 from New Radnor in the direction of Llanfihangel-nant-Meln and on the right hand side of the road there is a narrow little track signposted *on the left* as 'byway'; turn up there (it's very steep and rutted! but gets better on top) and eventually you come to the most enchanting spot with the delightful name of 'Water-Break-its-Neck'; this is, of course, a waterfall. At any time of the year this is a magic place but naturally in the wintertime the fall has more water coming down.

Fiona on top of Wimble.

The top 'hump' as seen from the other side.

SUGAR LOAF
(1,955 ft.)

February 18th, 1987

On a fine summer's day or in early springtime this walk can be highly enjoyable but it is not everyone's choice in wintertime! It can then be, and it was, very exhilarating. Leaving home at 8·15am in fine, dry but very cold weather we travelled down to Hereford via Ledbury on the A438; once through the town we took the A465 to that centre of so much glorious countryside – Abergavenny. As you pass through Pontrillas and so over the River Monnow, you enter Wales! The fun starts at this point because the day's adventure begins to take shape; for us it certainly did, with the unusual sight of a cormorant flying along the length of the river! Once one reaches the *first* turning to Llanfihangel Crucorney watch out! There is another turning just a little further on (a half-moon shaped road that is the other end of the first turning!); pass *that* turning and almost immediately there is another right hand turn which leads to Panygelli – here the Landranger series 161 is essential for accurate navigation. Go on along this back road that skirts Abergavenny, pass Ty-Gwyn Hall and Llwydu Court, and so into a very narrow section that eventually becomes 'Chain Lane'; continue to follow this round the hill (having invisible Sugar Loaf on your right) until you cross, on steeply rising ground, a cattle grid. Over that and there is a sign on your right to the National Trust Car Park beneath Sugar Loaf. You can either park there or at one of the safe stopping places on the way, well off the road. Whichever you select you will have some 3 and a half to 4 miles to walk to the top and *not* to be recommended on a misty day – it is not as straightforward as one might think!

Fiona (my Golden Retriever whom I never do a trip without!) and I stopped at one of the lesser stopping places and as she examined every square yard of the hillside I changed into walking clothes and put on the pack. Taking a careful bearing we set off up the incline with Sugar Loaf nowhere in sight. On reaching the plateau above, another bearing, and from there the car and car park spot were now invisible – this is why it is a safe walk most of the time but can be dangerous, in poor weather, to the inexperienced. It had taken us an hour and a half to get there from home and some 47 miles. Around, from that first plateau, we could see Blorenge (1,833 ft) of our first climb and the Brecon Beacons (of which we shall hear more later!) and a whole area around us of majestic countryside and hills, most with a good covering of snow; what should we find on top of Sugar Loaf?

The walk is lovely with gorgeous views opening up on all sides and of course, once on top of that first plateau there stands Sugar Loaf, seemingly a long way off and high above one! The snow we later encountered at the top was not yet visible but the clear air, the sting of the wind and the lovely sunshine from a clear sky was winter hill-walking at its very best. We went along the widest track so as to enjoy this situation (you *can* go straight ahead down the steep valley and up the other side!) and approached the hilltop from what otherwise would have been the direct route from the National Trust Car Park – Sugar Loaf is National Trust property and a real jewel too. We got to the top and the Trig. Point at 11·00am exactly and what a magnificent sight from there; right along the line of the Black Mountains, snow-covered, as was the north side of Sugar Loaf. On all sides there was beauty and we carried out our usual ritual of taking a photograph of 'us on top'! For the first time on these trips we actually met some other people as we drank our coffee and sat (out of wind!) absorbing the views. Remembering what I have said about being properly prepared in wintertime it was with some horror, rather than any amusement, that I noticed one was properly dressed for the trip but the three others – all youngsters – not only had thin anoraks but Personal Stereos and town shoes! As the clouds began to gather from the north I did mention that fine though it was now, things could change quickly in the hills – they laughed! I wondered whether at 65 they'd be around still, to enjoy it as I was doing?

We came down by the valley route which provided much welcome cover from the increasing wind; the now overcast sky made it seem much colder. Back at the car at noon and then round the hill in the car, to picnic looking at the snow covered Brecon Beacons some 15 miles distant. This time we wasted no miles on a detour home because in wintertime dusk comes early and we motored the 48 miles back to Malvern without stopping. This completed the third time 'On Top' in the new series of adventures and the highest so far. If you remember my closing remark of last week then we *did* have 'our daily bread' – our loaf! And she *did* have sugar (snow) on top too. A wonderful day out, and only 95 road miles the round trip.

At 1,995 ft. Sugar Loaf is entitled to have snow lying; well, on the side!

Snow lies on the Brecon Beacons as we climb up.

On top and snow lies on the Black Mountains.

The Black Mountains.

CORN DU AND PEN-Y-FAN
(2,863 ft.)   *(2,906 ft.)*

February 25th, 1987

Bearing in mind it was still wintertime an early start was essential for this climb in order not to be on top as the afternoon storms swept in. In 1965 that was the penalty we paid for such an error of judgement and as a result I well remembered the 'white-out' conditions that suddenly prevailed with frightening speed and ferocity. We left home at 7.45am for this adventure therefore and went by the most direct main road route to Brecon, on the A438 and the A470; we crossed into Wales at 8.50am and then over the River Usk after earlier crossing the Wye; both looking beautiful in the morning light. It was fine, very cold and frosty with a fitful sun which did nothing all day to mitigate the cold driven by a strong south-easterly wind. We reached the point from which we'd elected to start – The Storey Arms on the A470 (now an Adventure Centre) – at 9.30am with the Beacons in sight for the latter part of the journey and covered to almost halfway down in snow – a fine, majestic sight which we stopped twice to photograph!

OS map 160 marks the Storey Arms clearly (984204) opposite which there is a large car park; there is also another further down the road on the other side (with toilets provided!) from where one can also start this climb on a diagonal route to the top of Corn Du; we chose the more direct route across the road and over the stile into the National

Trust land of Blaen-Glyn and so steeply up the well worn track to the first plateau. It was without doubt bitterly cold and not a walk for the faint-hearted – it was winter hill walking with the challenges that that past-time offers. In fine weather and on a warmer day this is a long, but not over strenuous climb with time on top to go on to Pen-y-Fan and, if imbued with sufficient energy and time, to Cribin too, at 2,608 ft. Today it was very tough going indeed and even on the lower slopes under the snow-line it was force 5 wind conditions; Fiona did not appreciate her coat being blown inside out! However, we continued to the stile at the head of the valley and gratefully down the other side to the stream at the bottom, which was all iced up. Here, out of the wind to some extent, necessary additions were made to clothing and headgear as well as a stop for 'elevenses'. Now the fun began! We started up the long slope towards the summit of Corn Du and in a short time we had soon reached the snow-line where we paused to photograph the beautiful surroundings; then exchanged greetings with a young couple heading for the top and gathered our energies for the next part of the climb. The snow had become frozen hard and very slippery; it was just possible to find rocky bits on the track below the snow but it eventually became all frozen hard and at moments, in the strong wind, even worrying. This was fast becoming no place for the inexperienced and I had to take serious thought for Fiona; alone I would have donned crampons for safety's sake and because at 65 one is not as rock steady as one was in 1965! But today it was the ice that threatened us and with Fiona on the lead, we made a few more feet but about 300 feet below the summit we had to admit defeat – experience allows one to remember that the top will still be there to walk to on another day! Better to go down now than to be a liability

First stile on the long, long approach up from Blaen Glyn.

Craig Ewan Taf at 2,704 ft. as seen on our right as we climb on...

to one's fellows; so we slowly retreated; retracing our steps in what was an even less secure situation now we were going downhill. The wind was relentless. The sun had long gone and the afternoon clouds were gathering on the western side with clear indications of snow before nightfall. Safe though the climb had been it is still not one to be done unless one has a fair experience of winter weather conditions in the mountains; to those of us who have, it is a day to savour for a long time to come with, (or as today, without,) the actual top of Corn Du recorded on photograph! We would be back for that in the coming year, and hopefully, with Pen-y-Fan and Cribin as well; the view is quite beyond any adequate description but we will be there before long!

Once down and back in the car park safely we quickly got ready for the road again. Lunch, somewhat late, in the Forestry Commission area on the other side of the valley with a stupendous view of the tops around in their snow mantle and then off home by a slightly different route.

So far we had seen a buzzard, a kestrel and a sparrow hawk but as we returned via Hay-on-Wye we took the B4352 to Bredwardine having turned off the A470 at Glasbury onto the B4348 and B4350; map-reading here is vital if you are to enjoy the lovely return journey along the banks of the Wye. On high ground above it at one point we saw two Canada geese. Then past Moccas Park, Tyberton and Madley. Off this road are such superb Herefordshire villages, Churches and places of interest that one vows to return in the spring to amble along it's length to savour them separately but we had many miles to go, so in Madley we turned off to Lulham and Bridge Sollers and that small byroad brings one out by The Weir on the main A438, and that National Trust garden is a 'must' in the spring! What glorious countryside this is indeed. Home by tea-time and as we turned into the drive it started to sleet – we had made the right decision at the right time!

The turn-back point! It was sheet ice here and force 8 wind.
The party in front had crampons on.

HERGEST RIDGE
(1,394 ft.)

March 5th, 1987

This week it was not to be as rigorous as last time and this little known area outside Kington (*not* Knighton!) is easily approached from the passing A44 and using the Ordnance map number 148 the starting spot can quickly be found. It is a rewarding walk both for height and for scenery, offering a commanding view in every direction and taking in one or two tops that have either been climbed or are to be, in the next few weeks.

We (that is the Golden Retriever and I, of course!) left Malvern at 8·15am again opting for an early start because a weather change was forecast for the afternoon and this climb can be done of a morning, if you wish. By 8·45 we passed through Leominster and along the lovely stretch of road through Eardisland, Pembridge and Lyonshall – surely three of Herefordshire's loveliest villages? At Eardisland we were stopped by the ducks crossing the road where it crossed the River Arrow! Round Kington and once on the bypass (still A44), leaving Kington on your left, watch out for a signpost to *Hergest*; one drives alongside the Arrow here and then suddenly there is the sign, so beware. Up into the houses on the other side of the river and watch carefully for a turning on your right just *after* a sign indicating *Hergest Croft;* take this next little byroad to Hergest (both Lower and Upper) and eventually to Gladestry. If time and opportunity permits then a visit to Hergest Croft Gardens on your return will be very rewarding! But for now we set off along the narrow road to Gladestry and wound our way above the Arrow and then beside the Gladestry Brook; we were stopped for the second time – and this time by two red-legged partridges in the road; a lovely sight in the morning. Then at around OS 148 257548 we stopped for coffee and to photograph the lovely valley scene below; exchange greetings with the farmer and note that a small post on our left indicated we had entered Wales Powys, it said.

Just short of Gladestry there is a small lay-by on the left where the car can safely be parked; here we got ready for the climb which begins just further down the road on the right with a finger-post indicating a footpath for *Offa's Dyke.* This lay-by is quickly found if you find Llan-y-Felin on your map – it lies just beyond that. Then up the track passing Choughs' Cottage – would we actually see one of those lovely, rare birds up here? We took the track to the point where it breaks away from Offa's Dyke and branched right so as to get to the Trig. Point on top. In doubtful weather (and today was fitful sunshine, so no real problem) a compass is essential because the route is not straight and in mist you could come down on the wrong side of the ridge! Our journey was made delightful today as we kept company with two pairs of buzzards wheeling about over the moorland and making their presence clear by the meuwing calls that always sound so plaintive.

By just after 11 o'clock we reached the Trig. Point and paused for the traditional photograph before winding our way further along this commanding ridge to the ultimate high point marked Whetstone on the map. All round were the tops we had recently climbed such as Whimble in the Radnor Forest or were hoping to climb shortly such as Gwaunceste over to our left. The Black Mountains loomed large and slightly forbidding in the misty distance where we are scheduled to be next time on top – with Waun Fach dominating the skyline. Unfortunately this is not, on a fine day, a very peaceful spot, as it should be, because it lies on the to and fro route for jet training aircraft and the air is rent every now and then by the noise; interestingly though this never once seemed to disturb 'our' buzzards.

To change our route back we left Whet Stone via the Offa's Dyke path and took that route down to the road. It is a fine piece of earthwork which offers a commanding view westwards – as it was intended to do, of course. It gave us an easier walk down and we were back at the car by the Gladestry Brook just after 12·15pm and in time for lunch in the gloriously remote countryside bounded by Gladestry, Glascwm, Painscastle and Newchurch. If time is no object then the rest of the day can be spent on a meander through these lanes or by returning via Kington and stopping first to see over Hergest Croft Gardens. It is an area full of interest and quite unspoiled for those who like slower and gentler ways of life. We had to be back by mid-afternoon and so took the road to Newchurch from Gladestry, then on to Dol-y-Cannau and to Rhydspence, on the River Wye to join the A438 until it met the A4111 where we turned left to join the A4112 for Leominster passing all manner of lovely Herefordshire villages with none more regretfully (because we did not have time to stop!) than Weobley. Home at 3·00pm with just 100 miles motoring as it started to rain. Another top right on the Welsh border accomplished, and surely spring is round the corner because the roads were full of yellowhammers and the fields full of lambs – a lovely time of the year to be out.

May Hill
(971 ft.)

March 11th, 1987

When embarking upon a venture such as the ones in this series it is wise to have a hilltop in reserve in case the day is right but the weather is wrong! Such was the occasion that took us this week to May Hill in Gloucestershire but not too far from the Welsh border, over which we usually cross to find the next top. The day came at the end of a spell of very bad winter weather with heavy snowfall in Malvern and its surrounding area, but it was dry, sunny and cold. We set off for May Hill as the worst of the deep snow still lay west of Malvern and our proposed climb in the Black Mountains did not seem possible, there being two of us and one having four very hairy legs! Settling therefore for a lesser top we drove down into Gloucestershire via the 'back road' through Welland, Castlemorton Common and Corse. Off the A417 there is a small byroad just beyond Hartpury which is signposted to the Gloucestershire Agricultural College – taking that road leads one to Highleadon where a stop will surely be made to photograph the magnificent Tithe Barn just prior to crossing the River Leadon on a very narrow bridge. We were fortunate in that the light was perfect and photography was a joy. The road then joins the B4215 and by going left and first right one can reach May Hill's environments via Tibberton, Taynton, Glasshouse and Clifford's Mesne. A lovely drive, especially in the springtime but as we neared our destination our worst fears were realised – there was deepening snow everywhere, whereas we had none since leaving Castlemorton Common.

Leadon Tithe Barn.

The view from Perrystone Hill.

In Clifford's Mesne one must find the delightful little pub called The Yew Tree, for it is from there that the climb begins, to take advantage of the best approach and views. We drove on up past the pub until reaching the cattlegrid and passing the National Trust sign – May Hill is NT property. Parking the car we got out to survey the weather. Bitterly cold in the wind; light snow and mist everywhere! Down below on the main road it was brilliant sunshine and warm; but this is what climbing mountains or walking on hills is all about. Fiona did not mind a bit but we faced another winter's walk to the top and no views for us today. The track is straightforward but as there are also many such approaches it is wise, in inclement weather, to take a bearing and good stock of one's surroundings, or there would be a long walk back to the car if one came down on the wrong side! We walked to the top but so bad was the weather that no photograph was possible today and leaving May Hill's modest 971 feet behind us we went down the way we had come up.

On a fine day there is a glorious view in every direction and many of the tops that we had done or will be doing come into view in Wales. It is not a difficult walk and easily accomplished in an afternoon with a tea picnic or of a morning with lunch on top – unless one stops before (or afterwards) for lunch at The Yew Tree Inn, which is well worth that visit. It makes it a longer but more worthwhile walk if one starts from the Inn but again care must be taken to select a proper track to the top and an Ordnance Survey map is valuable – it is number 162 in the Landranger series. If it is springtime then a drive round May Hill from Clifford's Mesne through Aston Ingham and Luxley and back to Glasshouse is very rewarding indeed for everywhere there are masses of spring flowers and daffodils outside peoples' homes. This drive of course was not for us today and we left this beautiful spot on the Hereford–Gloucester border sad that we had not had the views this time out. If time is short one day then this is a good walk; a lovely top to explore and not many miles to drive. We hope to be back into Wales next week.

May Hill (Under Good Conditions)

At a later date

This beautiful and easily recognised hill is no great giant compared with its neighbours over the border in Wales but from its summit there is a view that rewards the climb and this National Trust property is surely a jewel. Its distinctive crown of conifers is eye-catching from so many points of the compass and people will often say to one, "That is May Hill", but without knowledge as to what lies upon and around it.

The trees on top were originally planted to commemorate Queen Victoria's Golden Jubilee and although subject to the harshness of the wind they have remained a commemorative clump of conifers ever since because they have been added to on similar national occasions. May Hill is also the place were the English Composer, Gerald Finzi (1901–1956) wished his Ashes to be scattered because like Elgar before him, he was deeply in tune with the glories of the Three Choirs countryside. It is, without doubt, one of the most beautiful, inspirational and dramatic places and no matter what the weather one can feel its atmosphere.

Walking to the top can appear simple – indeed it is, provided one selects a well signposted path from the little road that circles it high above the Severn estuary; but beware should you decide to venture up from the more open side above Clifford's Mesne and then find the mist descend and blot out all points of reference. Without a compass and in company with a dog it is easy to become disorientated and to lose contact with an equally disorientated dog! Worse still, try that exercise (at your peril) in winter-time with snow lying deep on the hill and the hazards could scarcely be worse if one was up on the neighbouring Brecon Beacons. This may seem stupid when comparing May Hill's 971 feet with Pen-y-Fan's 2,906 but our second visit to May Hill was in sharpest contrast. It really was a superb Spring day and everywhere looked brushed and. combed; the houses and cottages around the Hill all had a riot of spring flowers in their gardens and many had daffodils on the roadside as well. Taking the same route to the top we walked across the side of the Hill amongst the sheep and enjoyed the increasingly lovely views to the North. Then once on top it is a perfect place for a picnic and the views down the Severn estuary, as it sparkled in the sunlight, were beautiful. It was warm; there was no wind: and it was very difficult to recall how potentially dangerous the earlier walk might have been had we continued. It is this total contrast in conditions that so often catches people out when walking upon the hills. Not everyone likes to carry a pack, a compass and be properly shod when just out for a walk but on the hills even the most ordinary looking day can turn suddenly different; the higher the hills the more likely this is to happen but May Hill proved to us that it has indeed two faces and its winter one is gloriously and provokingly different from its spring and summer one.

Coming off the Hill this time we drove over the road to Newent and not long after leaving the village of Clifford's Mesne there is the exciting possibility of visiting The Falconry Centre. On the hills one often sees Kestrels, Peregrines or Buzzards with occasional glimpses of Sparrow-hawks or Merlins. Here in this Centre one can see them in working captivity for not only can you admire them at close quarters but there are flying displays and instruction sessions so that Visitors can see and learn more of our fine raptors. May Hill has much more to offer than just its clump of trees on top!

The top of May Hill.

Ysgyryd Fawr (Skirrid)
(1,596 ft.)

March 25th, 1987

This is the name that it is known by in Wales – more commonly known as *Skirrid* and looking like a young Matterhorn from a distance, and almost unclimbable from the face it offers to nearby Abergavenny; it is a climb for the athletic and strong, if you go by any route other than the one offered by the National Trust (whose property it is) which is by footpath from the B4521. We elected to climb this exciting hilltop from a little byroad off the main A465, Hereford to Abergavenny road. On a fine, clear spring morning Fiona and I drove down to Hereford from Malvern meeting little traffic at the latter end of March and got to our point of turn-off just beyond Pandy on the hour. The meadows beside the Monnow River were full of lambs and it was a glorious, early spring day. To find the right turning watch out for a signpost on the left for Llanteems, Llangattock and Llanvetherine – it is just before the turning to Llanvihangel Crucorney and Skirrid Inn which is on one's right – if you get *there* you have gone too far! Up the little byroad on the left taking the first even smaller turning on the right which leads to Pen-y-Parc and is unsignposted; at that point turn right and *do not* descend the hill marked 'Unsuitable for...'; now the tricky bit! As you proceed slowly along this lane you are actually circumventing Skirrid and if you watch *very* carefully there is a footpath sign hidden (almost!) in the hedge on your *left* just beyond a white house – OS 161 (Landranger series) ref. 333192. Opposite, there is a beautiful view across the valley to the Black Mountains from a double gateway in which there is room for a small car without causing obstruction to the farmer. We got permission from the house opposite to park there and then we changed, ready for the climb. It was to be very tough going; very, very muddy and the first three fields were full of newly born lambs. One must emphasise that this approach is for the enthusiastic hill walker and not for others as it is not a long walk but it is increasingly steep unless one selects sheep paths that go round the hill and go up in a series of diagonals; this is possible. Over the stile set into the hedge opposite the gateway and across the fields provided Fiona with her first encounter, at very close quarters, with young lambs. When one attached itself to her and nuzzled her she promptly sat down and licked it! Meanwhile

As seen from the lane turning.

mother ewe 'baa'ed vociferously in protest! We gradually left the sheep behind and through several gateways, over two stiles and we were at the foot of Skirrid Fawr; through the last of the gateways and one is face to face with the NT sign telling you that this is their property – if you find that sign you are in the right place! Looking up at the face of the hill now, you can see how steep it is going to be and if you walk round the base to your right then there is the rocky ascent and the view that gives it such an impressive appearance from a distance. We decided upon another of our direct approaches! It was hot, tiring work but we had one enforced stop halfway up as we sheltered between huge boulders from a passing shower – very refreshing! Having shared a piece of Kendal Mint Cake we tackled the next section and gained the Trig. Point on top by 11·00am – and what a superb view it is too. One of the finest all-round views in the Abergavenny area because one is just that bit nearer to the mouth of the Severn so that things are visible that are not from Sugar Loaf which lay across to our west. We could

As seen from the lane turning.

now see the other two tops that we had done recently – Sugar Loaf and Blorenge – and this hilltop of Skirrid Fawr makes a wonderful climax of the trio. Fiona ensured her photograph by sitting down by the Trig. Point which, on the face we then photographed, has a National Trust sign upon it denoting where you are.

There is not a great inclination to go anywhere after reaching the top but there is much to be said for taking a leisurely stroll along the ridge towards the far end and admiring the views; from the point at the far end you look down into Abergavenny and can see the less traumatic approach that the National Trust offers off the B4521 where, incidentally, there is a small car parking spot provided. As we lingered along this ridge and stopped here and there watching first a kestrel and then a sparrow hawk hunting, we also looked down into the cockpit of a passing Tornado fighter! In so short a space of time one is at a height that removes one from sounds below and one feels apart from the everyday world. It is hard to tear oneself away as well you may find if you do this particular climb on a fine day with plenty of time in hand to picnic on top, choosing a different view with each sandwich!

The return journey was uneventful but if you are careful, and it is fine (but *not* if it is misty or foggy, as I am always saying) one can descend by any suitable track and then walk round the hill to the starting point by the NT sign encountered on the walk up. This is rewarding as it gives various impressive views of Skirrid as she presents her differing faces to you. It is not difficult to re-trace one's steps, as we did, across the fields of lambs and so back to the car in 'our' gateway. For the drive homeward we took the same little byroads out until we reached the first side road that runs from the A465 to Grosmont over the top of Campston Hill; this is easily found on your Ordnance Survey map

161 and provides a lovely alternative route back to Hereford joining the main road and crossing the River Dore at Pontrillas. Opposite, at this point, is the road that leads to two more of Herefordshire's delightful villages, full of interest, Ewyas Harold and Abbey Dore; the latter offering an hours wander, especially in springtime, round it's Abbey and ruins with, possibly, a visit too to Abbey Court Gardens alongside where, last year (1986) we had the finest cream tea I've ever enjoyed! That road in turn leads one all along the River Dore and is best known as 'The Golden Valley'. Our schedule on this particular day did not allow for such delicious diversions so we headed back to Hereford and then via Ledbury into Malvern; a lovely day out on the hills and a climb that would be long-remembered and not least for the view it gave us of a very different climb to well over 2,000 feet onto Waun Fach in The Black Mountains at a later date – *see p.67*

Pegwn Mawr
(1,920 ft.)

March 28th, 1987

This adventure takes one into a very different part of Wales – a complete contrast to all that Fiona (my Golden Retriever) and I have shared so far in our attempt to repeat the climbs to various hilltops as were originally accomplished in 1965–1967; the challenge now being that I am 65 and we want to repeat the adventures before I am 67! Fiona is proving herself a most worthy successor to my original Black Labrador, Marcus, who did with me all the climbs in those early years. This particular walk or climb has a subtitle taken from a map name which appeared on the original OS map 128 and vastly intrigued me at that time – *David's Well* – still marked on the new Landranger series, No. 136, but alas! this new series does *not* indicate the exact position of the real Well; and there *is* one there, which the story in the prologue to *David's Well* (p.55) will prove, because on our way to climb Pegwn Mawr in 1965 we stopped on the road looking out for this Well and were entertained by an elderly Welshman, as the story relates. For this trip we went by the same route; we found the Well; we photographed it and we remembered with gratitude that amazing Welshman and the now long-departed, gallant companion, Marcus.

We were fortunate in that on this trip we had a whole day at our disposal, which you need really. It is a round trip of some 170 miles but the scenery, the various ranges of hills and the changing terrain make this long day out so very worthwhile. We left Malvern at 8 o'clock and went across country to join the Worcester to Tenbury Wells road – the B4204. It takes nearly half an hour through the lanes to get to Ham Bridge over the Teme just after Martley and there were superb views of the Abberley and Whitley hills on our right; and then up the hill to Clifton-on-Teme, leaving (regretfully) the ancient hostelry The Lion Inn behind, and on to Tenbury. The view on this road at the hilltop inn called 'Tally-Ho' is an inspiration to press on into Wales; we did; with the Clee Hills on our right, crossing and re-crossing the flooded Teme and once past Tenbury out onto the Prestigne road B4362 which took us past Croft Castle, a National Trust property well worth a visit on another occasion. After Lucton look out for a right turn (the A4110) which takes you up through the lovely village of Wigmore with the ruined Castle on the hilltop, to join the A4113 to Knighton. On this road, just after Bampton Bryan we crossed into Wales clocking 63 miles in just one and a half hours. It was here; back in the Teme territory (although for some miles while we had been in the River Lugg's valley) we encountered floods which brought our first diversion – not too serious and only adding quarter of an hour to our time. There then follows a most glorious stretch of road with wonderful views leading one into Knighton or Tref-y-Clawdd in Welsh, meaning 'The Town on the Dyke'; Offa's Dyke passes through the town and thereafter keeps one company throughout the rest of the journey, off and on. There are various ways to Llanbister but we took the narrow one over Bailey Hill which is high up, unfenced and has lovely views which afforded us the first sighting of the day of a buzzard, soaring graciously and dropping occasionally to investigate the ground. Map Landranger series 148 is essential for this trip and then on to 136 to complete your journey, as we did, to David's Well. Map reference is OS 136 059787 with the title on the map beneath that point – that reference is where the actual Well is situated and today there is a telephone box on that cross-roads. We delayed here and found the Well, with much joy, after all these years; a solitary, marshy place with no glamour or significance to indicate its presence to any Saints' Well seeker! But a remote spot full of history and meaning to me. I did not take Fiona to see it – only the reading of the original story will tell you why! We did divert up the road through two gates to the top of Red Lion Hill for our elevenses and were rewarded by peace and quiet; sheep in profusion and warm, sunny weather with superb countryside in every direction. From the top we could see our destination, Pegwn Mawr standing in aweful loneliness across the valleys some 5 miles to the north-west. Do *not* attempt to walk to it from David's Well even though there are tracks for part of the way; it is boggy, complicated and if the mist catches you, it is dangerous. I speak from that well-remembered previous experience when we set off on a clear day to do just that ... and then the mist came down and we were (for a time) well and truly lost in the open moorland until we picked up a bearing; in those days there were no Forestry Commission plantations in the area so it was an even wilder region with few points of reference.

Leaving David's Well we drove, and I recommend that you do too- to Bwlch-y-Sarnau and out towards Pant-y-Dwr but turn *right* at the 'T' junction and aim for Waun Marteg going on up that little unfenced road where today we had to stop and free a pregnant ewe, caught in a bramble thicket at the roadside. Having done that successfully we drove on this very narrow, unfenced and beautiful little road to a point marked on the map *Felin-Gytrhos* where there is a Chapel beyond which a farm road leads off to the right to join Glyndwr's Way. There is room to park out of anyone's way on this remote farm track and we met a farmer who gave us assurance that we would be no bother to him "provided that the dog is no bother to my sheep" – I assured him that Fiona was a model of good behaviour and we got ready for the long haul to the top of Pegwn Mawr.

This walk, for walk it is and nothing like the climb of the previous adventure to Skirrid, begins by following the track from the farm to the top of Pegwn Bach or alternatively one can go via the track to the *left,* denoted clearly as part of the Glyndwr's Way, which in turn leads one to the flanks of Pegwn Mawr and then onto a track going for the top and the Trig. Point at 1,920 feet; from there, after a walk of about an hour or so (depending upon how often one stops to admire the increasingly beautiful views) there stretches out before the eye one of the more spectacular hilltop and moorland scenes of Mid-Wales; it includes much of places already visited and holds within its panorama many spots yet to be visited in the months and year ahead. This is an area of amazing richness both in topographical terms (it possesses many tops that are quite unvisited by the more cautious) and in terms of flora and fauna. We were driven off the scene on this occasion by one of those capricious tricks of British weather – from bright sunshine it suddenly started to snow! So down we went seeking both shelter and lunch. It stopped as suddenly as it began but by then we were back at the car and off to one of the many delightful, tiny lanes of the area to picnic beside a somewhat swollen stream, with lambs playing in the fields alongside and hazel catkins showing their first signs of green

That way! and what a view of Radnorshire.

First view of Pegwn Mawr.

life; with the sun out again it was indeed a gorgeous spot with the surrounding hills towering above us on all sides. You, like us, can find just such a spot on your return journey if you travel by Bwlch-y-Sarnau and Abbeycwmhir to the A483. After getting there we went across country to Dolau (with magnificent views from the top of 'Little Hill') and over the main road to join the A488 for home, where we turned *right*, heading for Penybont on the A44. This final stretch of the A488 affords what must surely be the finest all-round mountain and hill view in Mid-Wales and there are places to stop safely and admire this entrancing scenery. A piece of road that must rank with the best in Europe. Once at Penybont and on the A44 it is straightforward to drive home via *Kington* (and *not* Knighton, this time!), Leominster and Bromyard to Malvern. Our only interest on this stretch was finding that the ducks on the River Arrow at Eardisland had by now regained 'their' river, whereas previously they were swimming on the A44 after it burst its banks! A fine day out and at the end the trip meter read 177 miles as we turned into the drive at 5·00pm.

5th August 1987, A-top.

DAVID'S WELL

PROLOGUE
Cambrian Hagiology

September 1966

It was one of those glorious summer days when it was very hot, even at ten o'clock in the morning. We had enjoyed the earlier cool of the dawn by getting up early enough to drive into Montgomeryshire in time for breakfast. The inner man was satisfied at an ancient hostelry, and from that excellent start to the day we drove over the hills to discover a little bye-road (leading off the A483) just beyond Dolfor. We had not long left the main road when we overtook him; he was not conspicuous and indeed one took him for a shepherd, though he had no dog, which was odd. He stood in the middle of the road and signalled us to stop; we did. In broad Welsh tones he asked, in English, whether we were for 'David's Well?' Then he saw my companion and said he was sorry but he thought I was alone; he wanted a lift. We would have taken him but the back seat was piled with luggage, and of course we did not know how far David's Well might be. Our destination was a hilltop some 1,920 feet above sea-level some miles to the west of the road, so we drove on, saying how sorry we were. A little further on we planned to leave the car in some convenient out-of-the-way spot and start walking.

The map said that 'Pegwn Mawr' was some three miles off the road if we stopped at the cross-roads we were approaching – good! We'd be on top easily in time for lunch and what lovelier day to see the view than today. We anticipated an exhilarating walk over the fields and on up the long approach to the hilltop; past streams and woodlands. Then we saw it. It stared at us on the map in large letters just at the spot where we'd planned to park the car – *David's Well.* He would catch us up shortly and there we would be standing, changing into walking things, with one sock on and one sock off, he would come along … we parked quickly; changed in rapid time – at least I did! My companion stood ready on the road. "Found it then" said the voice; "Not much of a place really but it's powerful, man; I come every year to take a bellyful and never had a days illness in my life". With that courtesy that the Welsh people show, he never referred to my failure to transport him to the spot, nor did he refer to my apparent knowledge of the Well, which to him it must now appear I'd come, with my companion, to 'take the waters', you might say. My heart sank for we would not be off now – not for some while I could see. So we walked across the field with him to the Well and when we got there, somewhat the wetter as we tramped through the deep grass and rushes, he suddenly shouted with joy: "Ah! there it is; been here every year all through my life. I live in London now, with my daughter, but I come back every year to drink David's water. Clears the system you know; never had a days illness in my life". With that, he bent to the Well and took a glassful of the precious liquid in a small sherry glass he had taken from his pocket; but again the old-world courtesy came out and he offered me the glass first, as his guest. I wavered only for a moment – I hoped he'd not seen – and then I downed it at a gulp. "It'll not kill you, man," he said as he drew another glassful. Grateful that the ordeal was over I turned to look at the place. It was only a small pipe coming out of the ground as it rose a little from the damp field bottom where in full wintertime there must be a stream. Today in high summer there was only a soggy area surrounding the pipe and from the hole came a trickle of water to add to the brackish pool immediately below. From the pipe and not, mercifully, from the brackish water, he drew. Then it happened again – here was the second glass before my eyes and my companion stood leering at me from a discreet distance. "Good health," I said somewhat stupidly; and all I got for that was a remark to the effect that David's water was precious. "Why man, when they tried to take over this meadow some years ago now, to build council houses, do you know what happened?" Of course I did not. "He held back his water until they changed their plans; as soon as they went away we were alright. This was the only place for water when I was a boy and we walked here from those houses, where you passed me by a while back." Informed now and also chastened for not having given him that lift, I started to take my leave telling him of our proposed walk. Time was getting on if we were to be there and back by four o'clock, as we must.

"Fine dog you got there; bit scurfy though, along his back." My companion looked saddened at this revelation of his personal problem and moved away a little as if embarrassed. "Do you drop him in the well now," he said "and it'll all go, you'll see." Well, that was it, of course! "Come here, old dog" I said, and as he trotted up to me I bent down and stroked him fondly. "Drop him in, man" came the voice tinged with impatience. The awful act stared me in the face. The trusted companion of my many walks, in all his black beauty and with that look that labradors have, was now to be dropped, yes *dropped,* into that dirty, brackish, soggy pool that lay beneath the Well's mouth; the thought that my host might take hold of the dog if I did not, was all that I needed to make me take action. Bending down again, I shot my arms through his legs and gathered the other two in my hands and in one swift movement inverted the old dog into the pool with a splash that covered me in mud and water. I jumped back; my host roared with laughter from the bank whence he'd retreated to be out of range. The dog … where was the dog? … he's gone! Drowned! … I've drowned him, I thought; but in a moment he shot to the surface with all the noisy spluttering that a full-sized dog can command. He shook himself and gave me a look that I shall not forget easily. "Again, again – do it again!" said the man on the bank; and so off I went and gathered the great dog into my arms and staggered back to the pool; wet now and smelling to high heaven, I was. *Splash!!* the deed was done. "Come on up now, man, and have a drop," he said as I recoiled from the wetting and gratefully I climbed out of the watery mire and stood beside him on the bank above the pool downing a third glass of this 'precious liquid'. I felt that I owed this to my beloved animal; if he'd to bathe in the stuff then the least I could do was to drink another glass out of companionship and loyalty. We moved on after that and I never saw my 'host' again.

It may seem silly, but we walked better that day than we've ever done. All the obstacles – and there were many more than we'd anticipated – seemed to fade before us and the heat was delightful. Lunch on top of Pegwn Mawr was delicious and the view from there is truly magnificent and well worth the effort involved. You can see right along the coast up to Snowdonia; you can pick out, on a clear day, the various ranges that lie between – Cader; the Rhinogs; the Arenigs, and Snowdon herself towers in the distance. Given not only a day like ours but also a start to the proceedings such as we had! He may be there again this year, if he's still alive and if he is I wish him well and 'Good Health' – in my own particular way! He will have his drop of liquid and I mine but he will leave behind him two happy souls, for it is a strange truth to tell, but told it must be, that since that day I've lost my indigestion and my companion has not a vestige of scurf along his back. We will be back there one day to walk again and I'm not at all sure that David's influence will not be pretty strong – at least on one of us!

DAVID'S WELL REVISITED

July 21st 1999

It was the morning of July 21st in 1999; it had a strange 'feel' of being different this time: do not ask me why, but the seasoned traveller to 'out-of-the way' places in Wales feels it in his bones! Up at 5·00am and off in the car by 6 o'clock, I travelled by Fromes Hill (where I sighted Wales in dawning fine weather) and so on to Leominster and onto the A44 signposted Rhayader. I turned onto the B4357 for Knighton where I allowed myself to enjoy breakfast at an Hotel. After breakfast I set off again for my destination – David's Well and a sight again after many years (1966, the previous story!) of Pegwn Mawr and its farm below where I'd asked the Farmer if I could walk to the hilltop with my beloved dog, Fiona.

On this re-visit occasion the first confirmation of those 'feelings' I'd had became obvious – it started to drizzle. It did not promise well for the day. Secondly, I got lost because the directions given me by someone at the hotel were inaccurate and by now so was my old OS 128 map! So using the more up-to-date 147/8 I unwound the 'directions'. I solved the complicated problem and eventually picked up the route of 1967 and of 1987 as I halted for a huge flock of sheep that passed just as I'd gotten the right road along to David's Well. Delayed then by conversation with the Shepherd I found time was slipping by and my premonitions about the day seemed to be becoming more real by the half-hour!

As I drove down the well-remembered road to the Well I realised, with shock, that my original host (of the well water episode) had had his worst fears realised – *they had built rows of bungalows* just where he used to live in a small cottage. I drove on saddened and my worst fears deepened. I came upon the crossroad and the Well itself – not now visible but a huge overgrown meadow of rank grass and water weeds and there was no way I could see it or even get to see it had it been visible as of yesteryear.

I set off across the moorland road intending to call at the Farm below the hill of Pegwn Mawr and see (for old time's sake) the Farmer who had been so understanding on previous occasions. Passing Bwlch-y-Sarnau, Pant-y-Dur and Felin-y-Gytros, the road was still very lovely and hereabouts unspoiled; I found the farmhouse but alas! Emrys was away at the Show Ground in Builth Wells; I learned this from their neighbour with whom I left a message for him learning that he had now retired and the Farm was worked by his Son. I had known, over the time, Grandfather Emrys, Father Emrys and now there was Son,

Emrys. Very Welsh and at last something positive on this otherwise depressing day. As I took my leave for home the sun came out; I drove slowly homewards stopping to picnic on a certain seat by the ruins of Abbey Cwm Mir and finally over the hills and through the valleys to Malvern. In all this had been a longer trip of 183 miles in all, including the diversions! It seemed strange not having Fiona with me.

Above: The meadow.
Right: The source.

Black Mixen
(2,135 ft.)

May 7th, 1987

It did not require an idyllic early summer morning to provide one with an excuse to travel down the A44 once again, outward bound from Malvern for New Radnor, not too many miles inside the Welsh border. Our destination on this occasion was the remoter hilltop of Black Mixen, up the same valley approach as that walked in an earlier climb when, in winter conditions we tackled Whimble. Leaving home at 8·00am we managed the 51 miles to New Radnor in one hour and a quarter, because the road was virtually without traffic. The beauties of three villages through which one passes were beyond adequate description – Eardisland, Pembridge and Lyonshall have to be seen to be believed, especially in blossom-time and on such a morning as this, with a milky haze in the distance heralding a warm, sunny day to come. The chestnut trees were in full candle and the air coming into the car through the sunshine roof was heady with the scent of blossom. A day indeed to be out-and-about!

As readers of the Whimble article will know the approach to this climb is via that enchanting lane (clearly marked, on the far side of New Radnor) as Mutton Dingle; this is a steep approach and very narrow indeed, so beware! Up to the very top and straight into Forestry Commission territory where, at the entrance, one may park safely.

Fiona was ecstatic at being let out and impatient as 'Master' got his boots on and got the pack ready for the long walk and climb ahead. Then it was off up the track leading out of the forest on the left – do *not* go on up the forest track itself. Once out onto the moorland the track ascends alongside the forest and at the end of that particular plantation Whimble comes into full view on one's right. A photograph on this glorious morning was a good excuse for stopping and regaining one's breath, but the pause is more than well worthwhile because behind there is the view to the right of Gwaunceste Hill (of which more later) and to the left there lies the Hergest Ridge (the subject of an earlier chapter). This morning all this looked magnificent and the air around was filled with the call of hundreds of sheep and their lambs. Now the climb begins and to reach the top of Mixen you must follow the recognised grass track that leads on into the valley; this is the next

Half-way pause for elevenses.

The track to Black Mixen.

Little Creigau and Harley Dingle to the Great Rhos.

valley to Harley Dingle where ammunition is tested by a company and is 'out-of-bounds' as notices indicate on your way up our valley, on your left. The tops of Whinyard Rocks and Bache Hill lie on the right of this track and the heights of Great and Little Creigiau keep one company on the left with a very dramatic steep valley between. The bilberries were coming in to flower and so was the heather. It was halfway up this steepening ascent that we saw our first buzzard; then a cuckoo flew by to land quite unperturbed on the post beside the track but most striking of all was the sound of hundreds of skylarks rising out of the hillsides as we walked by. As the track nears the top of the pass there is a gate beside which there is a hilltop pool and here we paused for our elevenses to be entertained by the antics of several pairs of wheatears and patience rewarded me (and not us, because I did not let Fiona near!) with the finding of one pair's nest. It is a spot to enjoy at leisure on a fine day and enjoy it we did to the full.

It had taken us about an hour to reach the gate at the top of the valley and so it was time to move on; to get to Mixen from here you must take the track on your left through the gateway and go up by the electricity post on the hilltop; the line of posts that have climbed the valley route with you stop here and the electricity goes underground, supplying power to the relay station on the summit – at present out of sight. Following this track round the hillside brings one to the moorland on top and soon the sight of the masthead; the Trig. Point is alongside but being that much lower is not visible until one has traversed the moor quite a bit further. We reached this point around midday but it can be done quicker if one goes directly there, or slower if one stops more frequently to enjoy the scenery and absorb the stillness of the mountain sides. At just over 2,000 feet there is a clear view now over to the top of Great Rhos (2,166 ft.) which in times past was the finest hilltop in the area to climb but is now in forbidden territory being map-marked as 'Danger Area' due to the activities of the valley testing far below and which extends onto the Great Rhos, alas. The Trig. Point is clearly visible on such a day as ours and so is the one on top of Bache Hill on the other side at 2,002 feet. Indeed on a good day and with time available there would be no more enjoyable walk than to climb, as we had done, to the top of Black Mixen then turn around and walk over to Bache Hill, descend into the valley and on up onto Whimble and home via the forest track to one's car below. Today we slowly re-traced our steps choosing a spot with the best view for lunch and photographing our achievement before leaving the summit.

Depending upon one's time schedule there are a variety of ways home or there is tea to be had in a real English teashop in Eardisland – what finer way of ending a day out in beautiful Wales than to have tea beside the River Arrow on one's way home? It was a day worthy of that sometimes overworked word 'serendipity' – the unexpected was pure joy throughout this walk.

On top again, Black Mixen.

WAUN FACH
2,660 ft.

May 13th, 1987

Magnificent, is today an overworked word but in terms of sheer beauty and majesty of surroundings there can be no other adjective to describe the 360 degree view from this summit. It is the jewel of the Black Mountains' range and on this day the weather was both fine, dry and with sunshine from an occasionally cloudy sky, so that the shadows were superb and the long-distance views enhanced. At the summit cairn one is rewarded with all the tops, both near and far, and it takes a while to name them all. The temptation is to stay and gaze upon so much loveliness without regard to time!

Our route outward bound from Malvern was the familiar one (as for Skirrid) along the A465 from Hereford. This time of the year we passed hedgerows dripping heavy with May blossom and passed valleys thick, in places, with bluebells. At the Rising Sun Inn watch out for your turning on the right to LlanFihangel Crucorney which once you've successfully taken goes down under the railway but be sure you then turn *left* opposite the telephone box in Stanton. You want the road to Partrishown but do *not* turn onto that narrow road to the village but continue, as sign-posted by the Forestry Commission, into the Mynydd Du Forest. Here the road becomes quite idyllic and there are plenty of stopping places and picnic spots alongside the River Grwyne

Fawr which flows out of the reservoir of that name at the head of this valley. Continue, as we did, on up the valley to the top where a farm gate bars your way to further motorised activity! Parking here is no real problem but turn round first or you may be too tired to negotiate that tricky business after the climb! We did, and on leaving the car were rewarded by the sight of four buzzards and a pair of grey wagtails and then … yes! a dipper; this delightful and not easily found little bird (due today to stream pollution in some places) kept us company for the next quarter of an hour as I got ready for the climb ahead.

The route from this top picnic site (and parking spot) is *over* the river and over two stiles to clamber up the steep track immediately on the right of the sheep-wire fence that borders the forest at this spot. You should have the small feeder stream to the Grwyne on your *right* and the fence and forest on your *left*. Up this track. This time I make no apology for the fact that it is a steep, long and perhaps for some, tiring climb but there are plenty of places to pause and admire the growing view behind and eventually as you get higher there are several plateaux on which to rest and enjoy your Kendal Mint Cake, coffee or whatever takes your fancy on such an expedition! We found time to do just that and then began the long haul to the top of Waun Fach. This is around a mile away and just some 36 feet higher than the top of the tump of Pen-y-Gadair Fawr and you may prefer to remain there, if the weather has been wet recently! The reason is that the ridge track is very, very boggy and although the views of all sides are superb the going is not! On a fine day and when the track is hard it is a lovely stroll to the top but Waun Fach is *not*, surprisingly, marked by a Trig. Point; instead there is a solid piece of stone and a small cairn on black, peaty ground. Nothing like as romantic a spot as the top of Pen-y-Gadair, but it *is*

River Grwyne – the road in to the start.

On top of Waun Fach.

Pen-y-Gadair (2,624 ft.) en-route to the proper summit!

the highest point on the Black Mountains. We got there and back in an hour having delivered our three stones to the cairn (one for each of us and one for absent friends) and then we thought that we'd used our last photograph of the film! but there was just one to record Fiona at the summit on this occasion! Back at Pen-y-Gadair we stayed on top of it's tump for a long time taking in this breath-taking panorama of hill and mountain tops. It had taken two hours from where we parked the car. On a fine day this is *the* place to eat your lunch and glory in all that nature has to offer. The reservoir below is just visible but what takes one's breath away is the sheer number of peaks that are to be seen from this mountain top. For the rest, you have to do the climb yourself and provide your own words of wonder and I only hope that you are blessed with a fine day such as we had, so that your pictures may provide you with a lasting memory of the grand occasion.

We descended by the route we'd come up but it *is* steep and going down is never easy especially to untrained muscles so take it gently and watch out for wet muddy patches which can be dangerously slippery. Once back at the car we had our tea and sitting by the stream were again fascinated by the antics of 'our' dipper who was plainly feeding young nearby in a nest in the overhang of the stream. The route home is your choice but we returned as we'd come, via Hereford. It is 9 miles from the reservoir (your parking spot) to the village of Llanfihangel Crucorney and then 27 miles back to Hereford. In all it is some 50 miles each way from Malvern. May or perhaps September are the months that make the valley most attractive and it is *not* a climb to be recommended in the wintertime except to the well experienced hill-walker/climber. A day that (now very tired!) Fiona, and I, will long remember.

Gwaunceste Hill
(1,778 ft.)

May 21st, 1987

On the old version of the Ordnance Survey map (number 128) this delightful hill was easily identified as being 'just above the 16 grid line'! That was as good a way of indicating it to someone not well verse in map references, as any other. On today's Landranger series (number 148) the reference is 158556, being the Trig. Point on top. That is where we set out for from home (in Malvern) on this occasion and a most superb day it proved to be. If previous walks and climbs have provided wonderful views and panoramas, then this walk stands out as the finest all-round expedition; it offers views of valleys, woodlands, villages, farmland and upland, near hills and distant views of hills and mountains; all in one a breath-taking walk. It is a walk to spend time over and not to be rushed and it differs from previous expeditions in much of what it has to offer by way of journeying also.

We set out on the usual route to Hereford and from there via the A4103 (for a change) until that road joins the A480 at Stretton Sugwas and then onto that road up to Lyonshall; here one joins the more usual A44 and so on to Kington and New Radnor leaving previous climbing places on one's left and right (Hergest Ridge, Whimble and Black Mixen) until the Forest Inn turning (signposted to Builth Wells) on the A481. Pause at the marked parking spot (a blue P on your map) and take a careful look at the birdlife on Llyn Hellyn – usually very rewarding. Then on down this road until one reaches the *second* turning on the *left, after* the one on the right to Frank's Bridge. This is a farm road which is tarred for the length you require to reach a suitable parking place; but it is very steep and often strewn with tree branches and populated by sheep! A mile up it gives out onto a track and here there is room to park off the track and we asked permission of the shepherd, especially as Fiona wanted to show she was obedient! We were received with the customary Welsh kindness and told to have a good day on the hill. We had driven 57 miles and done it in one hour and 35 minutes. The day was fine, dry and chilly with much cloud but this gave one superb photographing conditions. Ready at last for the longish walk to the top we noticed no less than six buzzards above us;

and around, the most beautiful views of the surrounding hills, especially the Carneddau above Builth Wells. Here I spent much time in my schooldays whilst my parents were abroad and maybe that accounts for my love of the hills, and especially in this area.

The map is essential in order to keep accurate direction so as to reach

Finally, the top.

the top of Gwaunceste. Following the track initially and through the gate up onto the down where heather and bilberry grow in profusion, you leave 'Giant's Grave' on your right, then you proceed along the side of the Forestry Commission plantation for it's length until reaching the little tarn named on the map, Llyn-y-Waun. Here we watched a pair of lapwings courting and the display was fascinating – the lake was almost dried up and there were places where it was stony; territory to the liking of this declining bird due to the ploughing-up or over-planting of its usual habitat. We took note of this pair as it was the 'lapwing watch' period. Then on over the heather and up the track to the Trig. Point on top of Gwaunceste. What a view! After the formalities of photography (for Fiona's sake, of course!) one was able to identify (and on a good day so would the Reader of this tale) the distant Malvern Hills, the Black Mountains, the Brecon Beacons, the Radnor Forest, the Hergest Ridge and so on. It is not so majestic as, say the top of the Gader Ridge and Waun Fach, because some of the hills are nearer and more intimate but the combination of near hills, distant mountains and descending valleys on all sides, together with the colours of the cloud bespeckled sunlight, made this a memorable occasion. Larks and linnets were everywhere and one was hard put not to tread on a nest and there was much evidence of partridge and grouse. The only sad disturbance to this haven of quiet and peace was the fairly frequent intrusion of the low-flying jets; however much they may annoy us they do not seem to disturb the animals because later we met two riders who said their horses were now quite used to the sudden scream and indeed Fiona no longer crouches as she used to, in fear. We took our time both up and down; on a fine day it would not be hard to find one's way but do *not* be misled, as I often say, on this sort of territory if there is mist about. What may seem a straightforward walk up can suddenly turn into a nightmare return if you are caught on top without your compass and map. We turned eventually, for base, and once at the car planned our route home.

There are many ways of returning to Malvern but this one is special! Going down to the main road again we turned left and past the 'Hundred House Inn' then took the *first* turning on the *left*. Drive, as we did (and if you are in no hurry) along this lovely little byroad through Cregina and go on down until you come to the even smaller turning on the left to *Rhulen*. Here you will find the most superb little Welsh village Church in perfect condition and much cared for, in a setting that is out of a fairy story. The primroses were still out on the banks and the bluebells in the hedgerows; the rooks were building in the trees at the back and the sheep were calling from the steep hillside

Llanbedr Hill.

all round – it was pure enchantment. We rejoined the road (only three quarters of a mile detour) and elected to go over the mountain road to Painscastle which is shown as a dotted yellow road on the map going over the top of Llanbedr Hill. Quite thrillingly beautiful (on such a day as this was) and a place to rest awhile. We saw a badger! And then our second pair of lapwings and a curlew. Almost heady with excitement, enjoyment and contentment we very regretfully set course for home once down into Painscastle where the road drops down into Clyro and so onto the A438 to Hereford. The region on the south side of the A44 hereabouts is so very well worthwhile for not only are there many tops to climb or walk but it is also a mine of jewels in lanes, rivers, villages, churches and suchlike. We shall return to it at a later date.

Postscript

There is another method of enjoying the long walk to Gwaunceste and this is from the village of Glascwm which on map 148 lies just below the grid line 16 that runs up to the hill itself. From Glascwm there is a path through a gate beyond the telephone box which climbs up the valley and onto the ridge at 'Giants Grave'; from there the route is as before. The day we did that route we drove back over Llanbedr Hill and saw a red kite! A most rewarding and glorious part of Radnorshire.

The Church of St David in Rhulen, The Valley of Vale; unspeakably beautiful.

Buzzards, Red Kites and Sparrow Hawks own the land here.

Picnicking on Llanbedr, looking over to Gwaunceste.

The view from the top of Wapley Hill.

WAPLEY HILL

(1,000 ft.)

June 1987

If, as once before in these notes, you should find that time or weather or opportunity prevents a longer outward journey then as well as May Hill, this smaller hill, at just on the one thousand contour, is very rewarding indeed. It is on the top left hand corner of OS map 149 (345625) and is within Forestry Commission territory. Travelling from Malvern via Bromyard and Leominster, take, as we did on this occasion, the A44 as far only as the Kingsland turning, the A4110, and go up to Kingsland itself turning left there to Ledicot and Shobdon. It will be well worthwhile trying (and that may be the operative word!) to find Shobdon's Church because it is worthy of a visit being highly unusual – I will say no more! It lies within parkland through which one drives up to Shobdon Court – marvellous in daffodil time. From there take the B4362 road out of the village and go only as far as Combe Moor; there, opposite the Post Office, is a small turning which climbs round the hill to the plantation know as The Birches. It is possible to park there on open ground, safely off the road. We then walked along this road until we reached the entrance to the main forestry plantation and where the map marks a footpath; this one can follow to the top of the hill and onto the Fort marked on the very top. There is a gate through which one goes behind a private house and then up onto the Fort itself; the best and most rewarding view however is from the cleared part of the plantation (and remember it may be replanted by the time you read this!) to the west, where one has an uninterrupted view of the countryside and hills to the west and north with the Malverns coming into their own on the horizon.

There are several ways of descending and it is possible to enjoy a ramble inside this Commission area; the bird-life is also exciting, depending upon the time of the year of course. On the descent it is well worthwhile, upon joining the main route down, to turn right and walk along round the hill westwards because you will surely pause, as we did and ate our sandwiches, enjoying the most superb, uninterrupted view of the Brecon Beacons. At any time of the year this is spectacular but in wintertime when they are snow-capped it is special. This is then a safe walk and not a demanding one but to get the best from it one needs a clear, fine day. Because of its location and its apparent lowly size it might never attract your attention but if you find the right day then I do not think you will be disappointed. The area around Wapley is some of the loveliest in Herefordshire.

PART II

The second in the series of adventures by one man and his dog in the hills and mountains of Wales, undertaken twenty years after making the journeys originally.

PREAMBLE

Those who have now read the first part of this series will be familiar with the circumstances which led us to the adventures and discoveries contained in this second series of articles. Let me just explain: during 1965–67 my dog and I walked or climbed 76 hill or mountain tops in Wales, on my days off, outward-bound from Worcester at that time. Now that I am 65 it seemed an interesting idea to try and re-discover these hills and mountains before I am 67, and in company with my dog again. Not however the same beloved dog, of course, for he died, full of years, after many exciting adventures. The present companion of my travels is Fiona, a Golden Retriever, who is three years old and a very worthy successor to Marcus who was a black Labrador. So now, after finding our ways into and out of Wales; up to the top and down again on twelve very different hill-tops in the first series, we set out to find interesting routes, by road and by foot, to other hill-tops, some of which many people never discover and which are thereby unfrequented and undisturbed by the tramping of many feet. The natural world is therefore richer in these areas and the few nature notes that appear in the text are not a record of *all* that one might see but sufficient, I hope, to whet the readers' appetite! Similarly, the routes we take on our travels are not the only ones but are certainly the less frequented and the more interesting, in the main. There would also be more places and buildings or interest in these areas than just those mentioned in the text. Finally, we do not expect you to find the hills exactly as we did because the time of the year can make a vast difference and so can the weather! At whatever time of the year and under whatever weather conditions you walk or climb your chosen hill-top, we both hope that you enjoy every minute of your day out of doors. Please remember to be properly clad and do not forget to carry a map and a compass – the higher hills can be very deceptive for the unwary at *all* times of the year.

Gilwern Hill
(1,446 ft.)

The choice of this hill as the first expedition in the autumn of 1987 was dictated by its remoteness (and thereby free from late holiday-makers!) and the fact that for those who have read my first Series of 12 climbs and walks to hill-tops on and around the Border Counties of Wales, this journey will be familiar as it is largely along the A44. It was a beautiful September day as we left Malvern at 7·50 in the morning but our passage to our chosen destination was not as smooth as we had hoped; first, taking the B4214 (off the A4103) to Bromyard we were reduced to sheep's pace as we followed a large flock outside Munderfield; it was good to be brought up short in such a fashion as it allowed us to enjoy the scenery the better! Onto the A44 eventually and away to Leominster noticing as we passed the King's Head in Docklow that the enormous colony of House Martins that nest on the eaves of that Inn had not yet flown: indeed there was so much coming-and-going to the nests that they were almost certainly rearing the late brood which is sad because they may never be strong enough to migrate with their parents. Preparations for the annual migration were in hand elsewhere because we saw many Swallows lining up on the telephone lines the other side of Leominster. In spite of delays we got to that town by 8·40am and headed straight for *Kington*, still following the A44.

This beautiful road takes one past familiar hills of the first Series, such as the Hergest Ridge, Whimble and Gwaunceste until the junction with the A481 at Fforest Inn where one turns left on to that road, sign-posted Builth Wells. As I have mentioned before be sure to stop shortly after taking that turn and look for interesting bird life on Llyn Hellyn on your left – there is plenty of space to park off the bend in the road. Then down the A481 to the Inn named Hundred House but do *not* take the small road on your right almost alongside but continue on to the next right-hand turning, signposted *Howey* and *Llandrindod Wells* and with another sign below indicating that the road is 'Unsuitable for heavy vehicles'! Here the fun begins! Following the signs for Howey you pass through a farm and on up onto Gilwern Common going over a cattle grid as you climb. The scenery becomes breath-takingly lovely as the road gradually climbs to the top of the pass and just before reaching that point there is a stony trackway on your right which is where your walk starts and where there is plenty of space to leave one's car safely off the road and the track, by selecting a flat spot on the Common. After parking, the second part of the 'We' of these tales of adventure into the Welsh hills and mountains, jumped out of the car-boot delirious with excitement and glad to be free after the journey that had taken us two hours and ten minutes and recorded exactly 60 miles. The sheep and the traffic hold-up in Leominster accounted for this longer travel time; but I must explain – jumping from the boot was my Golden Retriever, Fiona, who will be familiar to anyone who has followed our adventures in the first series; she is a very beautiful 3 year old lady! In the sunlight, as I got ready for the walk ahead, she quartered every foot on the ground round and about and by 10·15 we were ready for the 'Off'. There were sheep everywhere, so be warned, should you likewise have a canine companion; Fiona is completely sheep-trained and very reliable in open country but Welsh farmers (especially the hill farmers with sheep on the high tops) do not take kindly to dogs that roam. As I have often said before if I meet or see a shepherd or farmer out on the hills I always ask if it is alright to take Fiona across their land. We have never been refused permission yet but this courtesy costs nothing and does much to preserve goodwill on both sides for everyone.

The trackway (and it is a proper metal track) takes one to the very foot of Gilwern Hill and can safely be followed along its length, as we did. Our leisurely walk along this track was soon halted by the first sighting of a Kestrel; then a little further on a Buzzard and finally, on the walk in, we saw a Raven. There is much else in this remote area for the lover of the countryside, both in flora and fauna, and it is well worth taking one's time over the walk. After passing through the second gate the track climbs to an eventual bend to the left with another gate; *do not go that far!* just as the track bends to the left there is a grass track on the right which takes you to another gate (out of sight at that time) which gives access onto the approach to Gilwern's Trig. Point at 1,446 feet. The reward for this walk is evident once you reach the top and as we performed the usual ritual of photographing Fiona by the Trig. point we enjoyed a panorama enriched by the colours and the clouds, which included Great Rhos, Black Mixen and Whimble; then Gwaunceste, Hergest Ridge and Llanbedr with the Black Mountains in the background; then Aberedw Hill, the Carneddau with Mynydd Eppynt beyond; and of course so much else. I mention these as some will be familiar to readers, possibly, and some will feature in future expeditions in this series. With such a feast of sights a very leisurely elevenses was called for and some further photography in what was excellent light. As we sat drinking in this panorama a second Buzzard came and sat on a post just some 30 yards away; in total silence Fiona and I watched this beautiful bird of prey whilst its mate circled overhead 'Meuwing' mournfully. On our walk back to the car we were treated to an explanation of this behaviour – their baby was on another post and was obviously learning the craft of hunting. Such are the joys of walking in the lesser known Welsh hills and although this was rather special there were nevertheless many other species around us including some gorgeous Wheatears. Alas, apart from sheep, cattle and some ponies we saw nothing four-footed but both Fiona and I could strongly smell *fox* on two occasions!

This walk is not strenuous and is safely undertaken even in poorish weather conditions although the view would not be so rewarding. After rejoining the car one can take a variety of ways home and although I often indicate an interesting one to readers, on this occasion I shall only mention that should you return the way we came then there is a lovely tea-shop in Eardisland and a stop in that village is a must, both for that, and to see the ducks on the River Arrow in what must rank as one of the loveliest villages in Herefordshire. Because Gilwern Hill is in such a beautiful place and Gilwern Common surrounds it with views in all directions, I feel sure that a longer day than we had on this occasion at our disposal is what most people would wish for and it is an area calling out to be picnicked in and re-visited at other times of the year.

Maps: OS 147, 148 and 149 (Landranger series) with useful information on the older series 128.

Gilwern – the objective.

Success! Fiona at the top of Gilwern Hill.

Cefn-y-Blaen and Red Hill
(1,264 ft.)   *(1,666 ft.)*

22nd September, 1987

If you manage to select a perfect September day and have a love of getting up early, then these two hill-tops are for you! The first is 1,264 feet and offers a minor panorama of most of what you are in for in part two of the day's climb. On Red Hill you are at 1,666 feet and the difference of just 400 feet is truly amazing. Fiona (my Golden Retriever, with whom many Readers will now be familiar!) and I find no problem in early rising and so we were away not long after dawn into a cold, misty September morning with cobwebs linking the strands of the blackberry bushes and the smell of autumn in the air. We had planned a full day out on the hills of Powys: one as a prelude to the other, though there is no reason why either should not be walked without recourse to moving on to the second, of course. We left Malvern by the A4103 which we picked up at Storridge and so to Hereford. From the top of Fromes Hill we had the most exhilarating view of the territory we were to explore; this panorama is certainly one of the most inspiring on a clear day and with the mist in the valleys it looked quite superb beneath a clear blue sky. On the outskirts of Hereford one can pick up the A438 (taking the A4103 still as a 'ring-road' round the outskirts of the city) which leads eventually to Brecon. Following the Wye was pure delight and the early sunlight glinting on the water was an added temptation to stop the car frequently and admire the scenery all along this lovely road into Wales. At Rhydspence, which one has to be careful not to pass, by being in too much of a hurry, there is a turning on the right up beside the Inn and after taking that turn one has to be very careful to *fork left,* initially signposted to Newchurch; pause hereabouts to absorb the views! Then keep left following the signposts for Painscastle and drive around Cefn-y-Blaen as your map will indicate; as you climb in the car so the view increases in majesty across the Wye below; on such a September morning it will not be difficult to imagine what we saw. Fiona thought she ought to get out at one point and was not a little confused to come almost face-to-face with something she had never seen before – a fox! He had been hunting, as the rabbit he held firmly indicated.

This first walk, to the top of Cefn-y-Blaen is very well worthwhile; it is not at all strenuous and provides a marvellous backdrop to the day, if you are attempting both summits, as we were. The way to the Triangulation Point on top is via a gate on one's *right* which in turn lies on this byroad opposite a single sign-post to Painscastle and lies at a fork in the road, where eventually you go to the right. One can leave the car on the wide grass verge here and walk through the gate up a good track through the fields, to the top. As we did so the view became more and more glorious with the Black Mountains for our nearest company across the Wye valley. In the fields we were crossing there were hundreds (I mean that too!) of mushrooms but as we were out all day we left them to grow but of course the temptation remained! On top at 1,264 feet the 360 degree sight of hills and mountains takes in not only the Black Mountains but also the Brecon Beacons, the Llanbedr Hills and the Radnor Forest hilltops that have been described in the first of this series, but also one can look back to the Malvern Hills, which seem to increase in stature as one moves away from them. Sheep and larks in profusion kept us company – nothing else. In the early morning this is surely a most wonderful place to be.

Back at the car we took the same road, as for Painscastle, but from now on you most certainly do need your map (OS 148) because it is tricky to say the least, if you are to find what we did. At the next cross-roads turn right for Rhos Goch and once down in the valley bear *left* at the fork to join the main B4594 road. There turn left and immediately right beside the Heremon Congregational Chapel – it is a 'T' signed road and very, very narrow. Our subsequent adventures might put off the faint-hearted but the end result is so well worthwhile, I promise you. Up this road you are aiming for *Bailey Farm,* where they gave us permission to park safely out of the way, but before getting there we first encountered a Welsh motor accident – I say it like that because the laughter, the ribbing and the general laissez-faire of all concerned made this enforced stop (whilst it was all sorted out) more amusing than many a TV comedy. After quarter of an hour we were on our way again but not before one member of the group had come to the car and thanked us for waiting so patiently and added, "This is the most dangerous stretch of road in Wales – always accidents, boy!" Maybe we were now expected to retreat but many years of motoring and walking in the lovely Principality has made one of sterner stuff. On our way again and in a couple of miles to be stopped by a lady passing in a very elderly 'farm' car who said we were "to drive a bit slow, you know, there is a cow in the road" … we did, but as we were only doing 20 miles an hour anyway it was difficult to go much slower, but sure enough just round the next sharp bend there was a large black Friesian cow contentedly munching from the hedgerow and standing athwart the narrow lane. As the lady who had warned us of this bovine hazard had apparently got past so, presumably, could we? Horns, of the motorised kind are not of use and nor are flashing of lights; a different technique is called for in such lovely rural situations. Gently we approached her side and got the car's nose between her and the left-hand bank: then leaning out of the driving window I was able to administer a suitable 'thwack' coupled with guttural encouragements, whereupon she moved into the bank, facing us with a mouthful of bramble and a look of bewilderment. On we went. Nearing our destination now, we were fortunate to encounter the farmer walking along the lane and as we stopped we asked about parking at 'Bailey' and about the dog on the hills? Re-assured about Fiona's obedience and behaviour with sheep, he then gave us directions as to where to park in the farmyard 'out of the way, you know'! *But* – and here came the *most* interesting moment of the day so far – could we wait a bit, please, as he had a bull coming down the lane! Sure enough as we waited, with him in front of our *red* car, there hove in sight an enormous Charolais bull which seemed to take up the whole of the lane; would the red car prove too much of a challenge and would the farmer then find himself in the position of Matador! I quietly muttered to Fiona to keep silent at this apparition and prayed that we might live to see the top of Red Hill in two to three hours' time … that wait seemed like eternity but sure enough the bull turned quietly into the farmyard on our left and with a cheery "Diolch" (Thank you, in Welsh!) we were signalled on our way. Gratefully we came to the end of this lane but needed not to go down to the Bailey Farm because there was indeed room to park safely by the hedge where we changed and got ready for the climb ahead.

See full story in the postscript.

Mawn Pool – the joys to come after the Red Hill adventure!

Take care at the outset to study your map carefully because Red Hill is *not* visible from this starting point and to enjoy the walk to the utmost we took the track down to the farm and on through it to the grass way leading up onto the ridge above – it is quite a long, steady climb – and once there we paused for the views and to re-set course for our first stopping place, *Mawn Pools;* here, in company with three pairs of Mallards, we had our elevenses. It is a magic spot of peace and remoteness lying the other side Glascwm Hill and opposite Gwaunceste, of the first series. One can then track along the ridge and down to Doctor's Pool and so on a bearing (a compass is a necessity in this area, especially if the weather turns misty, so do not be caught out, please) for the top of Red Hill at 1,666 feet.

Once on top we had the most marvellous all-round view which meant that several photographs were taken which, naturally, included Fiona 'on top', once again! There were so many Buzzards that it was quite uncanny and the gorse was out in little odd places intermingled with the vast expanses of heather, also in bloom. The wildlife was so well worth enjoying and I'll not mention all we saw so as to whet your appetite for this spot. The walk down is straightforward and can be accomplished by taking the track that leads down to the lane below and, if you are careful, comes out just by the gate where you have left your car. A superb round walk; a healthy climb of modest proportions and an area of great natural beauty but leave time to enjoy it all and do not be hurried – we picnicked on top and from the time we left the car until we returned we never saw another person.

After negotiating the return run down the lane without further adventures we took the B4594 as we joined it at the Chapel, turning left and then taking the first of the left signposted Bryngwyn Church; there we stopped, as you must too. To admire the view from the Churchyard and to drink in the glory of this (yet another!) much loved Church.

This Church is open for your enjoyment; it is used by us for our worship; please do not harm it in any way.

Such was the greeting notice on the door. It is so beautiful, with a wealth of history that in its contents stretch back to the 7th Century and through poverty and decay has come through to the lovely and beloved spot it is today – enormous credit to its dedicated parishioners, surely. You can find so much in this area to divert your attentions but a visit to little Colva Church is another *must,* if only to try the real 'Echo' on the hillside, which Kilvert mentions in his diary on February 26th

1870. Directions for finding this exact spot are in the guide sold inside this superb little building. Tea perhaps by the Wye at the tearooms on the Old Toll Bridge at a point between Rhydspence and Whitney-on-Wye and so home, as we did, along the A438 to Hereford and then on to Malvern. A round journey of some 108 miles.

Maps: 148 and 149 Landranger Series with some useful help to be found in the old series number 141.

POSTSCRIPT
Going Slowly To The Top

It is not exactly correct to say, after a wet holiday in any part of our island, that 'it always rains in … ' and yet Wales does have that unenviable reputation! When the day came for us to discover the remote hilltop of *Red Hill,* in Powys, there were the usual premonitions about the weather and its suitability for such an adventure; it is a very out-of-the-way spot and even getting there presents an interesting navigational problem once one is off the A44. The day dawned misty in our valley and the omens were good at six o'clock; by eight it was clearing and by the end of breakfast the sky was blue and there was no wind; was it like that over *Red Hill?* Some 50 miles separated us and the Welsh valleys have more rain than the Vale of Evesham! Stopping briefly on the top of Fromes Hill, which is a favourite vantage point with a panoramic view over mid-Wales, we could see the distant hills bathed in a slight mistiness that augured well for the day ahead. We drove on.

The lane leading up to the farm was very narrow and hereabouts in Wales that means one is able to touch both banks from the car! Grass grew along the centre and the sign at the entrance led one to believe that it was a road-to-nowhere, which accorded well with what our Ordnance map told us. Our first indication that all was not quite as it should be was the noise: men's voices drifting into the car through the open roof but though well used to and indeed a lover of Welsh singing, this seemed to be no choral rendering but rather, a harsh account of points of view that did not accord with one another – in other words, up ahead men were on the point of a punch-up! Gently we eased the trusty Citroen round the next bend to see that, small car though it was, by no means could we proceed further – there had been an accident; well, Dai had mistaken the bank for the gateway and Emrys had mistaken Dai's ancient Land Rover for the narrow road to the farm – the result was unfortunate.

An hour later my companion, a Golden Retriever, had completed her detailed investigation of the banks along the road behind us; I had laughed until the tears ran down my cheeks; Dai and Emrys had exchanged more words than Dylan Thomas ever wrote and the language was interestingly basic whether in Welsh or English! However, eventually the van was man-handled back to where our car had been standing and the lengthy process of backing down to "the gateway you passed a bit behind you … " was reached, and an exchange of priorities took place; was my journey important? Well, yes it was because I'd come some miles in order to climb *Red Hill.* "Oh! Red Hill, you say? Well that's my place and you'd be more than welcome to put your car in the yard up a bit now and then walk from there; safe? Your car safe, you say? Well there's no one there except the cattle later on like, but that's not now: you leave it there man." So I thanked Dai and moved off, over the broken glass and on up the lane. In half-a-mile we met a lady in pre-war wellies and an ancient green mackintosh: she was waving her arms in the air and shouting "Cow … Cow … Cow". We stopped. She came to the open window and told us there was a cow in the lane and I could not get by; it was eating the bank and she could not shift it; she was (yes, you've guessed, of course!) "looking for Dai to help her get it back into the field; the silly old fool (not actually her word!) had left the gate unfastened." I sympathised. She ran on, shouting for him; we drove gently round the next bend and there in the roadway stood a large Friesian, munching joyfully on this unexpected late breakfast. Now Citroens are remarkable cars but even they are not usually meant for driving over or under large cows but as we approached her she turned to grab another juicy mouthful and in a flash I had the nose of the car between her and the other bank; then with a great smack upon her rump (aided by encouraging barks from the back of the car!) we shot past her without a scratch upon either cow or car! How the old happy, early post-war Rally Driving days came back to one recalling only that such an encounter would undoubtedly have been at dead of night! We were free of our obstacles at last and only another half mile to our starting point for the long climb ahead.

I do not know whether it is the unusualness of one's Welsh encounters or the amusement that they often provoke because of the under-statements that seem to surround the circumstances, but this particular day it did seem quite incredible that we should be stopped yet again before reaching our destination. Dai's neighbour was in trouble and as we approached the turning on the left to his farm, way up on the hillside, he came running down the track to the lane and shot round to the window saying, "Stop man … " and then a lot more! Smiling, I asked him what was wrong? By now I had almost reconciled myself to a day's entertainment rather than one of physical exercise. He told me that he had a bull coming up the lane ' to take his cows' and if I went on I'd run into him; I would stay where I was, I said, and as he leaned, a bit breathlessly, on the window sill there came into sight the largest Charolais bull that I'd ever seen! He was swaying slowly from side to side as his great bovine possessions acted like a pendulum and rocked him along the lane! "Fine bull there, boy" said the farmer; I agreed. Then the awful thought dawned on me … I was sitting *in a bright red car!!* Anxiously I communicated this terrifying thought to my companion; slowly, he said, "So … you … are … boy", and left me. The bull got closer: the trackway to the farm got nearer: the car now appeared in imminent danger and its occupants were becoming very frightened; to the guttural growl from behind I replied, sotto voce, "Shut up!" and then for good measure offered a large piece of Mars bar which successfully gummed up her growling abilities! Then he moved. At what seemed to me to be five seconds from point-of-contact between bull and car the farmer leaned out and grasped the huge tuft of hair on its head and steered the bull up to the right and it continued slowly swaying from side to side up the track to its waiting cows! "Diolch" (Thank you) said the farmer with a cheery wave; Da Iawn (Very good) I shouted back, and with that exchange of words we went our separate ways.

Red Hill's remoteness is a tonic at any time but after the traumas of the drive up the lane it seemed like heaven that day; the sun shone down; the heather was in bloom; the variety of sounds from the surrounding hillsides all combined to make it seem so well worthwhile.

Only Golden Retrievers can look at one as mine did as I went to let her out of the back of the car; she seemed to be saying "We've had quite an adventure one way and another, haven't we?" and so together we set off for the top of the hill and as we sat for a picnic on top, two Buzzards wheeled round and round, gently mewing to each other; this was why we'd come to Wales; this and the panoramic view around us. "Cymru – Diolch".

On top!

A blue-tits nest on Brynewyn Church door.

THE BRECON BEACONS
CORN DU AND PEN-Y-FAN
(2,863 ft.)   *(2,906 ft.)*

September 29th, 1987

No! we did not climb all of them! Just two tops – Corn Du at 2,863 feet and Pen-y-Fan (the highest point in South Wales) at 2,906 feet – and to get there from our base in Malvern we went up to Brecon by the Wye river and returned by the Usk; but again, not literally: The outward route takes one alongside the beautiful Wye valley just as the return route takes one alongside the equally lovely Usk valley. The former seen in the rays of the rising sun on a misty morning in September, and the latter seen under the rays of the setting sun of a golden September evening must surely rank as scenery of the finest that our country has to offer? In the first part of *On Top Again* it will be remembered that on the 25th of February 1987 we attempted these two peaks in the Brecon Beacons under snow and ice conditions and we (particularly the canine part of that plural!) were defeated by the sheer cold, the ice and the very strong wind conditions, so we wisely withdrew just some three or four hundred feet below the summit of Corn Du – "but we will be back there before long", is what I said at that time, and this account fulfills that promise.

The above is by way of introduction, now for the details; Fiona and I were up very early on what was to be a really superb September day – St Michael and All Angels, as it happened – and we drove the straightforward route to Brecon via Hereford taking the A438 and A470 to the new bypass round Brecon itself and turning onto the Merthyr Tydfil road (still the A470 actually) at the final round-about and down that road as far as The Storey Arms opposite which, on your right, there is a large car-park. We were there by 9·00am and it is some 75 miles; there was no one else in the car-park and I changed to the excited whines of my companion who could actually *see* a rabbit on the other side of the road! The selected route to the summit of Corn Du was exactly the same as last time and *not* the alternative route from what has become known as 'The Toilets'! Previously known to most of us as either Pont ar Daf or The Waterfall but the more modern provision of the public facility has added another, less picturesque name for that starting point. We crossed the road and went through the gate into the National Trust land beside the Storey Arms (an Adventure Centre nowadays) which is marked as Blaen-glyn. Then the route is demanding and steepens with every step; this is a full day's outing for some or half a day for others, depending upon what one does when reaching the top of Corn Du – marked by a large cairn and at the start of the climb quite unseen from below. If there is any doubt as to weather conditions you would be well advised to take compass bearings as the area is bleak and featureless should mist come down; personally I always take my bearings no matter what the weather because in the mountains weather can be very fickle and what is a fine day at one time can turn, with great suddenness, into unpleasant conditions the next. So on up the long first slope to the stile over the wire fence and a

The actual point of the winter's abandoned climb
(see Part 1, Corn Du and Pen-y-Fan p.30)

grateful pause there for two legged man but none such for four-legged beast! The mist we had encountered off-and-on during the drive up had now disappeared altogether and the view of Corn Du was exciting as indeed the weather conditions were promising, with blue sky and no wind; we stayed only long enough to photograph the scene and were then on our way down into the valley below. The trouble with this particular route is that you do have to take in a descent of several hundred feet *unless* you take the upper route across the hill you've just climbed and go on to the next stile to the north and cross on the map marked footpath, so going over Y Gyrn and on to the Obelisk; this is a less severe initial route true, but it joins the route we had taken eventually for the hardest part of the summit climb at the outcrop of rocks above Llyn-cwm-llwch. I personally like the route we'd chosen because it dives down into the valley and the stream and there is always a chance of some interesting birdlife there plus the excuse for a longer pause for coffee! On this, now quite idyllic, morning I am afraid the pause *was* for coffee and the gurgle of the stream attracted my canine companion who took a dip which very effectively drove off the birdlife! We sat in the sun and took our time because what lay ahead of us was not easy, especially with a full pack, binoculars and a camera; it is at such moments that one remembers that it Was that much easier 20 years before, in 1966 whereas now one is 66 oneself and full packs seem to get heavier! We got off to a renewed start and on up the long

The glory of the hidden pool of Llyn Cwn Llych.

Corn Du accomplished – now the track says, "on up to Pen-y-Fan".

'On Top Again'.

slope to the top but it does get steeper and steeper. The pauses can be justified by admiring the increasingly glorious views around at every point of the compass or, as in the case of one couple we passed, by sitting on a stone and reading the morning paper!! By 11·00am we were on top of Corn Du.

From this lofty mountain top there is so much to see that it would be needless to itemise any of it here as map number 160 reveals most of what you might wish to identify nearby, and unless it is very clear there is not too much to be seen in the far distance, as was the case on this morning; the further distance was misty; but our immediate surroundings were of supreme beauty and quite breath-taking, especially the view down onto Llyn-cwm-llwch with its changing colouring under the sunlight in and out of high cloud. It is a spot to takes one's time over and if conditions allow then sit on the four points of the compass and drink in the views at each one of them.

It is not demanding to take the downward and then upward route from Corn Du to the high top of Pen-y-Fan and Fiona duly sat by the National Trust's sign on the triangulation point to be photographed and for all the world her look at me seemed to say that "we'd made it", just as we said we would seven months ago in the ice and snow conditions. It is again a place to pause for a long time and drink in the views and the general mountain scenery, with your map to guide you as to points of reference nearby. One such is, of course, the top of Cribin at 2,608 feet: below one's present high perch. Whilst only some 300 feet below it is some distance away and constitutes either a walk there and back or there and down and round! We did not go on to Cribin as both dog and man had enjoyed the day so far and a more leisurely return with a picnic was called for under such superb weather conditions now it was past mid-day. So we took the route back to Corn Du and then tracked left onto the route that many people take up the long, long slope from the parking place by the toilets off the A470 just above the Beacons Reservoir. On the map it is not difficult to see that the path divides at Bwlch Duwynt and either goes on down or across the top to Craig y Byllfa; this latter diversion makes for a superb picnic spot especially if you select, as we did, to sit on the rocky outcrop of Craig Gwaun-taf, in the sun and out of the slowly rising wind. A marvellous end to the day on top.

By 3.30pm we were back at the car having descended in an entirely individualistic manner with a homemade route across the side of Corn Du to the Obelisk and then across the ridge and down to the gateway beside the Storey Arms. A very tired Fiona just managed to jump into the boot of the car and was asleep by the time I'd changed my climbing boots and clothes. For the return trip I chose to drive via Abergavenny so it was down the A470 to the second roundabout round Brecon and off onto the A40 passing the turning to Llangorse Lake, which is a point of call another time surely? Then leaving the Usk at Abergavenny we took the little road to Ross, the B4521, which is enchanting having so much to see along its entire route that it constitutes a day out in itself – it passes Skirrid, White Castle, and then an enchanting sign-post to a spot called 'Dawn of Day' – I will tell you no more; we had our tea up there! Down into Skenfrith with its lovely old castle and church and so into Ross. Much in that area to be explored indeed; but from Ross it was via the A449 to Ledbury and home. A round trip of 150 miles and a day out to be long remembered.

Maps: 149, 160, 161 and 162.

WOODBURY HILL
(904 ft.)

November 4th, 1987

It is not always the actual height of a hill that offers the challenge nor yet the reward for walking to the top; it is, quite often, the actual position from a topographical point of view: so it is with Woodbury Hill. Seemingly insignificant: out of the way and not even measuring four figures in height, but nevertheless a top that is so well worth the walk and the initial discovery in the heart of some truly glorious Worcestershire countryside. Fiona kept me company on the cross-country route from Malvern, as usual, and did not complain at the many twists and turns that the journey involves. It might be called the 'Lanes' Route' in order to get to Woodbury from Malvern! Bear with me whilst I describe this interesting route first.

Using Ordnance Map number 150 we left on the B4219 (the Bromyard road) which joins the A4103 at Storridge. There we turned *right* and followed that road into Worcester as far as The Fox Inn on Bransford Bridge over the Teme river; at that point we slowed right down (as anyone following this route would be wise to do!) because after crossing the bridge the first named lane comes up on one's *left* – Otherton Lane – and it is a steep, hairpin bend to get up into it! Safely up we watched the ducks in the meadows below alongside the Teme and there is a superb place to stop under an oak tree on the top of the rise from the main road. The route along this lane takes one out onto the A44, Worcester to Leominster road where we turned left, for Knightwick. This main road part of the journey holds many fascinations on the way passing turnings to two 12th century Churches – St Leonard's, Cotheridge and St Mary Magdalene's in Broadwas-on-Teme: both well worth a visit. The next bridge over the Teme is Knightsford Bridge and just before it there is a turning on one's right, the B4197 to Martley. We turned off up there and followed the steep rise that takes one to the top of Ankerdine Hill where, on the top, there is a parking place alongside a hill-top underground reservoir; we paused there and took in this magnificent panorama with the Malverns on one's right and the whole of the vale of the Severn laid out below. I will not spoil your enjoyment by describing further exactly what one can see from this vantage point. So on to Martley where, to enjoy a round trip in glorious countryside we followed the B4l97 still, signposted to Stourport. This road eventually joins the A443 in Great Witley and here lies something that will delay your start of the walk up Woodbury Hill! We paused in the village to visit Great Witley Church, as well as to give Fiona a run in the Park around the ruined mansion of Witley Court. It is a place so well worth visiting and if, like me, you have read Mr Robert Walker's book on the history of Witley Court and its magnificent baroque Church, you will be fascinated by all that there is to see. To get there one must first turn right off the B4197 onto the A443 and directions are clearly given thereafter. Do not be put off by the approach road to the site: I can promise you that the journey and diversion from one's main purpose of the day is so very well worthwhile. The Church, originally at Cannons in Middlesex, in 1720 was largely brought to its present site in 1747 and is unique, as one look inside will indicate and I do not think I would be wrong if I suggest that after reading this you will want to stay much longer than just for a 'look inside'! It is also remarkable that this small village is so enthusiastic and caring for its magnificent Church that it mounts, annually, a full scale Music Festival; to hear one of the great Oratorios sung here with full Chorus and Orchestra is an experience never forgotten.

However, we paused here, really for Fiona's sake and to allow time for some photographs, having visited the spot many times before. Then on down the A443 passing 'Hundred House' turning left onto the B4203 and one must then watch very carefully so as to take the *second* little lane on the left – 'Camp Lane' – which is best identified by 'Turnpike Cottage' at its entrance with an old pump in the garden; turning up there we parked just beyond the footpath sign, on top of the rise where there is room for a car off the roadway on the grass verge. It was exactly 23 miles to this spot from Malvern, not including the diversion into Witley Court, so it is not a demanding journey and allows time for the interesting diversions I've mentioned. Whilst putting on the right clothes for the climb up Woodbury Hill the Farmer came along with his dog and we were able to ascertain (as I always like to, if possible) that he had no objection to Fiona being on his land; then we were away with his words ringing in my ears – "it is truly a most beautiful sight from the top; I've been farming here since just after the war and I still love it at all times of the year."

So we came to the walk itself. I must warn the readers of this walk to the top that it is not easy to find one's way nor are the views from the actual cairn on top anything to write about; but the different views on the way are lovely and especially when the countryside is dressed, as it was for us, in its autumn colouring. The first quarter of a mile is steeply up through a meadow and the footpath is newly signposted by the Worcestershire Countryside Commission and stiles are properly accounted for with new arrows marking the way. The view across the Teme valley from the ridge one walks along once the initial climb is over, are glorious and stretch from Clee Hill to the Black Mountains. We resisted the desire to pick from the huge harvest of sloes and lost count of the many different species of fungi in the woods we passed through. There were many varieties of small birds and we came across a Kestrel finishing off a small rabbit. The path, once one is on the ridge, can be confusing but we aimed aright by walking *round* Woodbury Hill on its southern side and so came upon the wonderful aspect of the Malverns from their north escarpment. We continued round until the path leads one into the woods that now, alas, cover the whole of the top part of the hill. Passing in front of the farmhouse there is then a gate leading into those woods and the path goes on until emerging on a lane by another house; continue *straight ahead* there and through the gate in front; then just after passing several willow trees on the left the path ascends into the woods and goes right to the top of the hill. The woods being a mixture of hard and soft wood do give cover to interesting wildlife – watch carefully! Fiona's encounter with a dog fox proved most interesting! At the very top (for which one has to turn *left* when on the final crossing path) there is a large cairn with the initials JFCB in the centre; if you find this you are on the very top but, alas, there is now no view. To enjoy the various views around this ancient camp (the outlines of which are still visible here and there) one must walk the perimeter track and pause, as we did, every so often at the gaps in the trees or undergrowth. On a fine day there are many choices of spots to picnic and the Clock-tower at Abberley is the centre of one view; the Shelsley Walsh Hill-climb is the centre of another; the Malvern Hills is the centre of a third. It had taken us exactly one hour to reach the top from where we parked the car but it can be done quicker and it may be prudent to take it slower! After gathering some edible chestnuts and allowing Fiona to enjoy several late blackberries we made our way down.

There are several ways of doing this. One can descend by the way one came up, of course; or one can take the newly way-marked route through the pine woods and so come out onto the lane (Camp Lane) and then turn *right* to get back to the car. This route allows one to enjoy to the full the glories of the Teme valley patchwork below and identify the various places of interest in the near and far distance, with the aid of binoculars and a map. The third route takes one down the other side of the hill so allowing Abberley Hill to come into view directly ahead with the village of Great Witley immediately below. The hills on the right in the distance are the Clent Hills. You come, via this route, into Walsgrove Lane and so to regain the car turn *left* and when coming to another lane turn left again (which is Camp Lane) and your car should be just up the hill!

The return journey can be as interesting as the outward one and it may be that so much of interest has been touched upon that another visit to the area is planned; so I will include one or two items not to be missed. First, if lunch is what you seek in the area then a diversion off the B4204 (the Great Witley to Clows Top road) is well worthwhile for there, in Abberley village, lies 'The Manor Arms' where assuredly you will find, as I have often done, a most superb lunch at the bar. Having walked to the top of Woodbury we chose to return by following along

A massive Cairn adorns the top of Woodbury Hill,
but nowhere can one find out who 'JFCB' is.

the length of Camp Lane and enjoying its dips and turns, and the loveliness of the autumn colours, to the full. This is also a magical drive in the Spring because of the daffodils and, later, the cherry blossom on the hillside down into Shelsley Beauchamp. At the end of Camp Lane therefore be sure to turn right down the hill, thereby passing the entrance to Woodbury Quarry – and beware of the heavy quarry traffic! Once down into the Shelsleys a visit to both Churches is rewarding and a look, by foot, up the famous Shelsley Walsh hill-climb hill in spring-time is one of the things not to be missed. The road home led us out from these two villages onto the more main road crossing first New Mill Bridge over the Teme and then Ham Bridge. We joined the B4204 and drove into Martley and so met up with the B4197 once again. At this point there is a choice of road depending whether you wish to head for Worcester or for Malvern – both clearly signposted. If you do as we did and go home via Alfrick and/or Suckley, two charming villages, then you can also pass both Nature Reserves that are in the area – 'The Knapp and Papermill', just by the Old Storridge turning, and 'Ravenshill' which is opposite Lulsley Pool; here, depending upon the time of the year, there can be found Tufted Duck, Little Grebe, Canada Geese and especially in summertime, some glorious Dragonflies. To find your way through this maze of byroads I hope that you have provided yourself with O.S.maps 150, 149 and 138. If you are fortunate enough to still possess the old series of maps then all you need to know is on maps 130 and 143. So a lovely day out in the Worcester shire countryside ended as the sun went down a golden ball in what was promising to be a frosty sky and a cold night, but the glories of those views from the top of Woodbury Hill will long be remembered.

MOREHAMPTON HILL
(709 ft.)

November 17th, 1987

It was exactly a month away from the shortest day when this walk took us to the top of what is, by our usual standards, a very small hill. Never despising a hill for its lack of feet (or metres!) Fiona and I felt that on a cold but fine late autumn day this was the right hill in the right place for a short day's enjoyment. We left Malvern at 9 o'clock and went over the Malvern Hills via the A449 to Ledbury leaving this delightful Market Town, which has so much to interest a visitor, by the same road that goes on its way to Ross-on-Wye. This is surely a most lovely road with superb views right and left – Perrystone Hill on the right and May Hill on the left, to name but two; and then there are the Marcle Hills which stretch many miles to the north-west ending with a triangulation point on Seager Hill. As we crossed over the B2040 I recalled an earlier visit just up that road, in Much Marcle, to an amazing early English Manor House by the unusual name of 'Hellens'; this is well worth a visit. We reached Ross by 9.30 and took the dual-carriageway round the Town at the first roundabout but not before we had passed the enchanting signpost to *'Hole-in-the-Wall'* ... another diversion which you may like to explore sometime: a small bye-road that runs right alongside the Wye with plenty of grass verge to picnic in peace and solitude, if you choose the right day!

There really is such a place – local history affirms that it was the entrance to a passageway under the River Wye to the manor house; a route favoured by smugglers from boats on the River Severn.

Leaving Ross on the A40 and crossing the River Wye, with a beautiful view from that bridge up to the Town itself, one has to take the A49 at the next roundabout for Hereford, and go on along that busy main road until reaching the B4348. Using OS Map 149 now we elected to visit Kilpeck Church by turning left after Much Dewchurch. This is a fine example of internal and external decoration by the Herefordshire School of Norman Sculpture; I will not spoil it for anyone by describing its beauty further – it has to be seen to be enjoyed to the full. From Kilpeck we wound our way across country through Wormbridge to Cockyard up the Grey Valley and so to the trackway that leads to Newbarns Farm on map reference 391356. We took that track and went down to the farm where the Farmer gave us permission to leave the car in his yard and told us of the Right-of-way that leads up to the top of what is known locally as 'The Hill' – Morehampton Hill, though the map does not so enlighten one! Fiona was delighted that we'd arrived and we set off for the top as the sun came out in an occasionally blue sky. The hill is being replanted and so is not very beautiful but there were many little birds including several very active Wrens. Overhead were two Buzzards as we neared the top and once there, at the triangulation point, the view is quite breathtaking! Below lies the valley of the River Dore in The Golden Valley; across it is the whole phalanx of The Black Mountains. Today there were storm clouds beyond and they did indeed look as their name says, black: a truly formidable sight. On a fine day, in summertime this view is equally inspiring but the colouring is, of course, quite different. We had achieved this top by 11·30am including stops on the way. It is a gentle walk and provided one has remembered to ask the Farmer's permission, both to park and to use the track to the top through his land, it is an unusual hilltop. It was just right for our autumn day.

Fiona enjoyed the exercise and once back at the car we made for the little hilltop village across the valley named on the map quite clearly as *St Margarets.* Here is surely *the* place to stop and have lunch? We did. At 'The Sun Inn' right on the top of the hill with a delightful garden that in summertime one can sit in and enjoy the silence whilst gazing at the majesty of the Black Mountains that lie in front about 10 miles away as the crow flies. It is a most wonderful spot and those who looked after us (when we stopped there in the summer of this year) gave us a superb Ploughman's Lunch out in their garden. Today it was indoors! Then before you leave a visit to the Church behind the Inn is a *must.* The Rood Screen in St Margaret's is quite magnificent and dates from 1520 AD; do not leave without seeing it.

If one wishes to extend the day, as we did in the summertime, to a full day out, then from the Inn one should drive down the hill towards Newton but turn left for Abbey Dore and Ewyas Harold – the names in themselves draw one in that direction! This road (avoiding Bacton) goes over the top of the valley with glorious views of the surrounding hills and mountains. Here we stopped and on our way home on this trip we saw a Fox, three Buzzards, two Kestrels and a Little Owl. It is a place to stop and to walk on the road by the woodland alongside. So on down into Abbey Dore village and first to the Abbey Church itself; here in springtime there is a riot of daffodils and time will be spent wandering in and around the Church itself and the ruins. Round the corner lies Abbey Dore Court with its Garden, open to the public; and here in the summer we had the finest cream tea that I've ever had! Long may this piece of rural, out-of-the-way olde England last. By this time, on a full day's expedition, it will be time for the return journey and from Abbey Dore it is only a few miles onto the A465 that leads one back to Hereford and so to Ledbury and home. It was a round trip on some 80 miles through what is gorgeous Herefordshire countryside with a glimpse of Wales; a sight of Gloucestershire and a backdrop of Worcestershire. The sight of Skirrid, standing up like a huge 'Matterhorn type' peak against the storm clouds will be an abiding memory of this day's outing as will be the formidable blackness of the Black Mountains. At any time of the year this is a good hill to walk and provides the excuse for so much else in a landscape that is abundantly rich in so many things that we too often take for granted in England.

St Margaret's, Vowchurch.

The glorious (c. 1520) Rood Screen at St Margaret's.

TITTERSTONE CLEE HILL
(1,750 ft.)

January 13th, 1988

It had been a long period of very wet, foggy and muddy weather, in January, but it was not just the change in the weather that took Fiona and me to the top of this hill, it was Fiona's behaviour! One morning, about the usual time that we try to set off on our adventures, she suddenly came to me with my cap in her mouth – a quite unprecedented action – as much as to say that it was time we were up and about again. So man and Golden Retriever set out for Clee Hill or to be more precise, the Clee Hills. There are two such tops; Titterstone Clee Hill at around 1,750 feet and just beyond, to the north-east, Brown Clee Hill at around 1,770 feet; the latter is today the more beautiful because quarrying and now large aerials have sadly disfigured Titterstone. But do not be too dismayed because not only on top but around and below there are untold beauty spots to be explored, and this we did on the day Fiona lured us out into the early sunshine.

The Hills themselves lie on the Worcester/Hereford and Shropshire boundary and to get there we went the prettier way, but it is not the most direct which lies along main roads otherwise. Leaving Malvern by the byroads we headed for Martley – this is a delightful cross-country route through Alfrick and Knightwick, then over the hill at Knightwick with its superb view back along the length of the Malvern

Hills. Once into Martley we followed the B4204 to Tenbury Wells. You might be tempted to stay awhile there as it is a town full of interest with a most rewarding Church to visit and nearby St Michaels, the home of the School of English Church Music. Just outside the town, after crossing the River Teme you come, on the left, to Burford House Gardens; this is also the home of the fabulous Clematis Nursery – Treasures of Tenbury. Its garden, the nurseries themselves and above all the most interesting museum are all well worth your attention, sometime! We could not stay this time as we took the B4214 (on your right, just before Burford House Gardens) and up the hill to the village of Cleehill itself. Wasting no time here we took the left turn onto the A4117 and then turned into the third turning on the right which from Map 138 in the Landranger Series you will see leads to Bitterley Court with its delightful little Church behind. Here, in springtime, it is a mass of daffodils and a place of peace and beauty. We got here at 10 o'clock having travelled just 37 miles. There are footpaths from here up the better side of Titterstone and by taking one it avoids the worst disasters of the quarrying.

On top facing North-West; this panorama is laid out for one's delight. The Long Mynd and Wenlock Edge.

As the never ending boulders gradually came to an end,
this sight greets one on approaching the top.

It was a damp, misty and cold January day (our first climb of 1988) and we delayed the start for a while to let the mist on top of Clee Hill clear and the valley to warm up a little. Meanwhile there was lovely Bitterley Church to re-discover. Dedicated to St Mary it is Transitional in period but on a Saxon foundation; the only visible remain of that time being the Font; but the setting, the Church itself and its interesting Memorials and the sight into Parkland of Bitterley Court (next door) are all well worth seeing; and we did not miss the astounding Churchyard Cross dating from the 14th Century and so well preserved. The beautiful setting of and the Jacobean/Georgian house alongside (Bitterley Court) are quite magical in the Springtime when the daffodils are out.

Gradually the sun came out and we explored the surroundings on this lovelier side of Titterstone Clee Hill. First one can go up to Titterstone village or hamlet and walk on up from there; the signpost at the crossroads tells you which way it lies. It is not the best approach. Then there is the walk from the end of the Bitterley Church road where as the road bends for the last time before going up to Warthill Farm there is a footpath by the barn that leads right up to Stocking Cottage and thus onto the hill itself – a lovely walk in better weather, and there is room to leave your car in the valley below. After exploring this area Fiona and I got back into the car and set off on what is a most rewarding drive around the hill to where we eventually walked to the top. If you do as we did then take your car back to the Bitterley crossroads from the Church and turn right to Bitterley village and then right there signposted Cleestanton. On the sharp left-hand bend there is a trackway up to Bank Farm and Stocking Cottage which offers yet another approach on foot to the top of Clee Hill. Turning then right at Lackstone, after passing through Cleestanton, we took the next road turning on the right signposted Bromdon and Cleeton St Mary. We dawdled along this road, as surely you will too, for the views are superb. Marked on your map (138) and at the reference point 606788, there is a Cattle Grid; just beyond this, on the common, we parked safely and then walked to the top of Titterstone Clee Hill; you will see why when you get there! It is a different world on this side to what one sees from the south and west. Bracken, large stone clumps, streams and seemingly unending plateaux; the latter to fool one that the next 'horizon' is the top! It took us, in an increasingly bitter and strong wind, an hour to reach the true top and the triangulation point that lies beyond the Satellite Earth Station. There are several ways of climbing this fascinating hill that has so many interesting and varied features, but from here it is best to select your own route. We decided upon a well-used sheep track initially and then along a bit of a valley (to get out of the biting wind) and so onto plateau after plateau until we got to the huge 'Golf Ball' almost on top. The views are simply glorious and the day had by then become fine, dry and bright. In the sunshine we stopped to photograph Brown Clee Hill some 8 miles to the north and when, eventually, we reached the trig. point Fiona sat down and 'asked' to be photographed – her first in 1988! The Malverns lie behind: the Radnor- Hills to the west: the Long Mynd and Wenlock Edge to the north-west: the Wrekin behind Brown Clee and the great panorama of the Midlands, both industrial and rural 360 degrees around. It is a marvellous sight on such a day. English weather being what it is, especially at this time of the year, it then clouded over quickly and in a moment it began to snow! Yet another indication of how important it is to be prepared at any time for the weather's caprices when on the hills. We returned to the car and the shower passed.

It is not really sensible in an area of so much beauty and with so much to divert one's attention in both rural beauty and local interest, to try and climb Brown Clee on the same expedition. This therefore forms the basis of another article. We drove home via Cleeton St Mary and turned right at the junction just over the cattle grid to join the A4117 where we turned right again to get back to Cleehill village, having thereby completed the circumnavigation of Titterstone Clee Hill. The views to the east and south-east from this main road between Doddington and Cleehill are lovely and lay-bys are provided off the road so one can stop safely and admire them. At Cleehill we turned left onto theB4214 for Tenbury Wells and then via the B4204 to Martley. One passes on this last bit of the route home, the Tally-Ho Inn on the hilltop just out of Rochford – it not only has superb views from its lofty position, especially as the sun is going down, but is also a place worth stopping at should one feel in need of refreshment! A really superb day out and so well worth the effort in wintertime, for which of course, I have to thank Fiona, because in that wind I needed my cap!

The (out of place!) Trig Point – even Fiona looks disgusted!

BROWN CLEE HILL
(1,770 ft.)

February 22nd, 1988

As readers may know already there are two Clee Hills, Titterstone and Brown; the former has been the subject of an article already when Fiona (my Golden Retriever!) and I climbed it in January. Some eight miles to the north lies Brown Clee – a very different type of hill altogether and divided into two distinct tops of which the further one, known as *Abdon Burf* is the higher and has the ordnance survey's trig. point at some 200 feet below the 2,000 mark. It is very steep on the west side and wooded on the north and east; it lies within the estate of Lord Boyne and it abounds with a variety of wildlife. To further interest in this aspect of the hill the Estate Office in Burwarton offers an interesting leaflet entitled 'Brown Clee Forest Trail' at 30p which is the third in the series of Nature Trails in Shropshire published by the Shropshire Trust for Nature Conservation. The hill lies just into Shropshire over the northern end of the Worcestershire border. There are several ways of getting there and it depends what you want to see and what you want to do as the Landranger Series of OS maps will show you on number 138 – to the west lie lovely villages such as Stoke St Milborough; Clee St Margaret, with the longest ford (which is part of the Clee Brook) that I've seen for a long time! and then delightful Abdon, from which village the top gets its name – Abdon Burf. You can also drive 'inland' of these villages and come much closer to the hill itself, going through Cockshutford and Woodbank. Along the stretch of road between these two villages there are two approaches to the hilltop on well marked tracks and footpaths and if you proceed round the hill on either road to Hillside and Hillside Farm then the Forest Trail begins there going up through the woods and on to the top if you wish.

The morning that the climb to the top of Abdon Burf became possible it dawned a cold, clear and promising day and for this particular journey I selected the route that is different to the one Fiona and I travelled over to walk to the top of Titterstone Clee hill. Today, in order to see different countryside I went from Malvern (which is where home is!) to Worcester and out through the St John's area on the A449, signposted to Tenbury. Passing through Great Witley (mentioned in detail in an earlier climb to the top of Woodbury hill) and leaving the little village of Abberley on the right I chose the B4202 so as to pass through Cleobury Mortimer. If time ever permits then a visit to The Manor Arms in Abberley village is always well worthwhile! Not today though as we drove on through lovely countryside to Clows Top and across the A456. As one heads down the road out of Clows Top the Clee Hills come into view for the first time – Brown Clee on the right and Titterstone Clee on the left. It is almost a ridge but with lower ground between the two and with the two main parts of Brown Clee clearly visible. Joining the A4117 (Ludlow road) one turns left and into Cleobury Mortimer with its lovely shingle spire and much else of interest; The Town too is worth your time with the Talbot Hotel for a meal perhaps and an enchanting shop by the unusual name of 'Pets and Petals'. On then we went to our destination passing fields of new born lambs and in places great clumps of snowdrops; and so eventually (passing first the turning we needed) we went, as surely you will wish to also, up to Doddington and out past its little Church; over the cattle grid and there by the roadside is a plinth in stone with a copperplate map on top indicating what one can see in the distance from this lofty vantage point. It made, for us, a good stopping spot for coffee! The view if it is fine, embraces the Malvern Hills, the Black Mountains and much, much else. Back we then drove the way we'd come to take the first on the left, signposted Crumpsbrook and Cleeton St Mary; this turning is just by the 'Foxwood Bird Sanctuary'. At the next cattle grid we turned left again and were travelling along the road by which we returned from our first adventure in this area when we explored Titterstone Clee Hill. Now we passed the spot where we climbed to the top that day in January and went on towards Brown Clee Hill away to the right; in so doing we drove right through a farmyard on this narrow, very rural road and passed banks of snowdrops. At Wheathill we turned right for Burwarton – the centre of the Boyne Estate. In this village is the Estate Office where for 30p one can purchase details of the Nature Trail Walk. Alas, the Church has been sold and is a private residence – a very strange sight indeed. Passing The Boyne Arms and some 2 miles on we turned left for Ditton Priors and then left again almost immediately onto a very narrow road signposted Abdon and Tugford. OS map number 138 is essential for this enjoyment because it is a most enchanting drive and there is also the pleasure of the walks to the top of Abdon Burf; either via the Forest Trail (as marked on the map at 610870) or via a trackway further round the hill. We chose the one round the hillside following the road round to Abdon and where it met the narrower road to Cockshutford there is a telephone box: here

Fiona disliked this sign, so we went up another way.

Abdon Church.

we parked and as I got ready for the climb to the top of Abdon Burf (Brown Clee Hill) Fiona gratefully stretched her legs and ran round me with her customary enthusiasm.

This track, which commences on Map 138 at a reference of 585869, has the merit of going directly to the triangulation point on top whereas other tracks and paths meander round the perimeter and cross the ridge from further away. All have their merits but time was important today so we chose this one. Through the gate and up the track Fiona found her first rabbit and I was delighted to see why … she disturbed a Sparrow Hawk! On up the track with an ever increasingly glorious view across the Shropshire countryside. Alas, the sun had gone for a long time behind clouds and distant views were not good but the outlines of Wenlock Edge and The Long Mynd were clearly visible. So was Caer Caradoc Hill just outside Church Stretton. A study of the older Ordnance map for this area is interesting; it shows no aerial mast on the top of Abdon Burf but now it has not one but two such masts alas. We have to accept this under the heading of 'progress'! We got to the top and Fiona climbed onto the high base of' the Trig. Point to be photographed, as usual, and then one could see along the ridge of this ancient and interesting Hill to the Hill Fort at Nordy Bank, and beyond that to Clee Burf which has been quarried and carries a further disfiguration of masts. This is sad as the whole hilltop and ridge is a place of great beauty and peace but it is the price we pay for progress in the age of satellite communications. It was very much colder on top and we were conscious that we had now got to nearly 2,000 feet and were not surprised to find a large patch of snow! The keenness of the wind and the longer forecast suggested indeed that it might be "waiting for more". Our journey had taken a leisurely two and a half hours and we'd travelled some 35 miles of that by road to get to our vantage point. After another cup of coffee we descended to the car safely parked by that telephone box at the road junction. If one has time then from here one can explore the surrounding countryside to great advantage as there is much of loveliness and interest in Abdon, with its tiny Church; Tugford, with its 'Sheila-na-gigs'! and Clee St Margaret. The lanes in springtime are a joy to the unhurried driver and picnic spots are so hard to select as one is indeed spoiled for choice. We came home through these villages and then to Clee Hill village and down the B4214 to Burford; joining the A456 and then the A443 for our run back to 'The Faithful City', as Worcester is called. From there home to Malvern. A superb day out, in Shropshire largely, and one that can, with walks, be infinitely varied to one's choice.

THE LESSER HILLS OF
HEREFORDSHIRE TOUR

February 8th, 1988

It had been a period of unremitting wet weather and the uncertainties of more distant heights made this delightful tour seem suitable for the time of year in question – February. Using Ordnance maps 149, 161 and 162 it is surprising to the casual visitor (and sometimes even, the even more casual resident!) what pleasures are to be found in Herefordshire – it is a County of infinite charm and interest. This tour, which also combined several short walks to hilltops, was made on a winter's day when snow lay on the hilltops and frost was hard in the valleys; it was a day of sunshine from a cloudless sky but there was a biting wind – a day to be out in order to see what was stirring before what surely was to be another period of bad weather. So Fiona and I took the car to Ledbury and from there we 'played it by ear' with only one condition pre-set – that she (my Golden Retriever!) should have a walk every-so-often, even if we were not bound this time for the high tops of the hills.

From Ledbury, on the A438 (the Hereford road) we first took off for Putley via the signpost on our left about four miles out of Ledbury. Here we went straight up the hill ahead (and *not* to the left to Putley itself) until we came to the lovely remote crossroads marked 'Woolhope

Cockshoot' where we turned right and drove, in snow, all along beside Park Coppice under Seager Hill. A walk through these woods on an approved footpath rewarded us with a glorious view from the trig. point standing on 865 feet; as a winter's day walk it was delightful and the views back to the Malvern Hills from this remote and unusual spot is well worth the effort and, at times, the mud! We were fortunate enough to see two Fallow Deer in these woods – as good a start to a day of surprises as one might wish for, and Fiona was fascinated. It is worth mentioning here that should one not wish to complete a tour, as we did on this day, then lunch in the valley below at The Butchers Arms in Woolhope is a delightful and delicious way of spending any, but especially a winter's, day at lunchtime. A visit also to the remote, utterly charming and very privately positioned Sollers Hope Church will complete a short outing to this area of Herefordshire but if time allows then on to Brockhampton Church and a visit to How Capel Court would complete a day out; all of this is easily seen within a small area of map 149.

Come On! The track up through the Putley Woods.

We moved on for our tour by taking the road down to Hoarwithy where it is possible to cross the Wye river and as we did so we saw how near to flooding its banks it was! If you are strong-minded then you will follow our route but if you should weaken then turn sharp *right* over the bridge, signposted Carey and drive all along beside the Wye until you reach that delightful black and white inn named 'The Cottage of Content' and there ... well, we did not, this time! Instead, we went through the village and took the right-hand road to Llanwarne – this is a very strange spot and its unusualness may detain you, as it did us, including a look into the ruined Church; enough said to whet your interest! From here we climbed up to Orcop and so onto Orcop Hill, 961 feet. There is a track off another such in the village. What a view! but it was very cold and by then the wind was cruel so we did not stay.

By car again on the little road round these hills to Saddlebow Hill where the whole phalanx of the Black Mountains lay in front of us as we sat in the car and ate our sandwiches – well, Fiona had a piece of each of mine! It was fitful sunshine by now and photography was chancy but rewarding if you got the cloud right! It is a most impressive panorama and on a Spring day it should be a most delightful spot to picnic. On round this hill and suddenly there in front lies Sugar Loaf and then Skirrid, just outside Abergavenny. Both were snow capped whereas the higher Black Mountains had been entirely snow covered. We ended this hilltop tour with a visit to Garway Hill. This is also approachable by a trackway and stands at 1,200 feet, thereby giving us the highest point of our day and a truly impressive panoramic view to match. As we gazed at this beautiful sight and Fiona investigated the possibility of rabbits, I was able to watch, at very close quarters, two

Buzzards hunting; this was made more exciting than usual as the wind made their manoeuvres quite incongruous and at times they were both very close to me, finally setting down in a nearby tree so that through binoculars I had a very close-up view of these beautiful birds of prey. A winter's day, when food is of paramount importance to all wildlife, one often sees very unusual things, which make a day out so rewarding.

So, with four hilltops visited and much of interest either detaining or offering at another time to detain one, we got back into the car and set course for home in Malvern Wells going via another hill which will be the interest of another article before long – Aconbury Hill, 905 feet; this is also a hill fort and stands above the Wye valley with views out over Hereford on one side and to May Hill on the other. To get here you come off Map 161, which will be needed for the three hills just described, and back onto Map 149 driving via Wormelow Tump and across the A49 to Much and Little Birch; then in the latter village there is a footpath – but that is for another time!

How Capel Court.

Llanwarne's ruined church of St. John the Baptist.

Orcop Church.

Today we drove home via this spot and then down into Holme Lacy joining the B4399 and so crossing the new bridge over the Wye and turning left along the A4224 to Mordiford (with its lovely old bridge over the river) and right in the village up the steep hill into the National Trust property, Haugh Wood. This led us back down the other side of the hill over Broadmoor Common (where in summertime one can pick delicious blackberries!) to Woolhope; past The Butchers Arms and into Putley and so home through Ledbury. It is not a tour that would be accomplished easily in spring or summer times: there would be too much to delay one from a variety of interests but as a winter's day activity both dog and I judged it to be a great success and in all it had taken us a leisurely seven hours and we clocked just on 80 miles. Obviously this can be added to or subtracted from, depending upon how you use the maps (149, 161 and 162) and what you decide to do on your day out but it is fascinating countryside and the best of Herefordshire lies in this area, surely? The Fiona's of this world will not go short of space in which to exercise and. no one will return home without a camera (and a memory) full of delightful memories.

Sugarloaf from the approach to Saddlebow.

GRAIG SYFYRDDIN
(1,389 ft.)

March 30th, 1988

It was one of those gloriously sunny, not too warm but windless days in early Spring as we set out from Malvern to drive the 35 odd miles to our destination. The area is known by the enchanting name of 'Dawn of the Day' and to prove it the local signpost at the crossroads offers that delightful name as somewhere 2 miles distant. We took the A449 out of Malvern and drove on it through Ledbury down to Ross-on-Wye; this is a beautiful road with superb views of the Marcle Hills and later, across the valley to May Hill in Gloucestershire. Ross has a bypass which avoids the Town and at the third roundabout on it we branched off onto the A40 (the Hereford road) until it met up with the B4521 and turning left there we headed for Skenfrith. This too is a lovely road and increases in beauty as one drives along it. On this day everything looked 'brushed and combed' and the sun shone down on the fields of corn and pasture.

The River Monnow marks the boundary with Wales and there, entering Skenfrith, we passed into Gwent. Skenfrith is a place that detains one; it has a lovely black and white pub called 'The Bell'; it has a superb Church; it has a ruined Castle beautifully maintained and it now has a Motel, which offers all that a traveller could require. We did not stay because our journey was taking us to 'Dawn of the Day' some few miles further on and to give a useful advance warning of the turning one requires, there is a village named Walson just 2 miles prior to the turning. As we climbed the hill out of Walson the fields were full of lambs, primroses along the hedges and the small, wild daffodils in the fields everywhere. At the top of this hill, if you watch very carefully there is a small dwelling on your right named 'Chapel Bungalow' – the turning you require is immediately after that on your right. It is on the crest of the hill so one must approach it carefully but the local signpost clearly indicates it – 'Dawn of the Day' 2 miles. For those who like such things, using OS Map, Landranger Series number 161 it is on map reference 417195.

Here, as you turn right, the fun begins! This road is very narrow and the hill one drives up is steep and twisty; the increasingly glorious views mean that it must be a slow drive and there are plenty of places to stop and admire the views in safety. We drove on up and *over* the crossroads straight into the road marked with a 'T'; follow this road, which by its turnings, offers new and exciting views to the east and south, whereas previously one had been looking west to the higher Welsh mountains. Along this narrow road one comes to a farm, clearly marked on the gateway, Celyn Farm and that tells one that you are on the right road! On and on until on one's *left* there is a large forestry type gateway with a 'Do not light Fires' notice beside it. There is room to park here and the footpath begins at this point. The map reference on OS 161 is 413220. We had taken 35 miles in distance from home and just on the hour to get there, so for such a beautiful spot it is not far from home for us. A high pitched voice of excitement from the back of the car told me that my companion felt it to be high time to be allowed out! So attending to Fiona's needs first I opened the hatchback and let her absorb the joys around such as any Golden Retriever can find once let out of car confinement. As I 'booted and spurred' for the walk to the triangulation point on top of this hill I admired, as surely anyone following this route will do also, the glories of the views around – it is a place to pause and take stock. The footpath goes through a gateway and is stone based so excellent for walking and after a while it enters the forest land and gives one glimpses of simply heavenly views across the valleys to Skirrid, Sugar Loaf, The Black Mountains and much, much else. Today there was still snow on the tops of the highest peaks, but in sharp contrast, from the valleys below there drifted up the incessant baa-baa of the sheep and their lambs. Daffodils were everywhere and overhead two beautiful buzzards hunted the escarpment. This walk is easy for a start and after some time one comes to a clearing with the track going on ahead into the woods and narrowing very considerably. The map offers one an alternative at this point: ahead, along the track until emerging into the field and so up to the trig. point; or, turn left up the grass ride and over the fence into the field and thence along to the trig. point. The disadvantage of the latter, as we found – and Fiona was particularly baulked – is that a new set of fences with barbed wire as well as sheep wire now bar one's way to the top; this problem can be overcome but it is not made easy by any stile. What route one selects is ultimately rewarded by a 360 degree quite fabulous view and we ate lunch with one side of the trig. point for the back with each sandwich and so looked out onto hills and mountains, near and far, with so much else as well. Not a spot to leave in a hurry.

When eventually the mind and the memory had taken its fill of panorama, of snow-capped peaks, of wooded valleys, of the sun glinting upon the Severn Estuary, of fields full of sheep and their lambs, of hills that had seen us on top quite recently, then – and only then – it became time to move towards the car and home. The walk back can be varied depending upon the way one has selected for getting to the top. Back at the car the maps that offer alternative routes are 161 and 149. The choice of route home is something to savour for it can be via Ross; or via Skenfrith and a stop there for tea! and then on across the A446 and the A4137 to the A49; then turning right and immediately left go down into Hoarwithy and across the River Wye there and on to How Capel and in so doing one passes right through the middle of a piece of parkland with lovely ponds on the right surrounded at this time of the year with a blaze of daffodils; then round the gracious house – Fawley Court – and up the hill to How Capel. If tea is still a joy to come, then a pause can be made at How Capel Court to see the gardens, take tea and enjoy the exotic display of fabrics that the owner specialises in and which are for sale, as are things from the garden nursery.

From this point it is but a short step to cover the miles across the B4224 and up the hill opposite which takes one down into Much Marcle where the road joins the A449 and so on to Ledbury and home. This we have done many times and it is, especially in springtime, a most delightful route. For a none too strenuous day out (or even half a day should one so wish) it is so easy to drive and walk; it is also almost unbelievable that such a superb view and yet sense of remoteness is to be found just about 35 miles from Malvern. It was indeed an inspiring way in which to mark the coming of another springtime.

After the hazards of this climb even Fiona looks exhausted!
The view to the West (left–right): Skirrid, Sugarloaf, Pen Cerrig Calch.

The view to the East: The Black Mountains – what a superbly worthwhile reward!

CARNEDDAU
(1,458 ft.)

February 1989

One of the greater joys that retirement brings is the ability to select the best day for a particular walk, or climb; the day my Golden Retriever and I set off to become better acquainted with a compact group of' hills just outside Builth Wells was a late winter's day at its very best: the sun shone from a nearly cloudless sky: it was cold but not bitingly so: there were lambs wherever one looked and the hedges were showing signs of greening up with pussy-willows and catkins in abundance. There was snow still on the tops of the higher hills but not much left on Carneddau. This little group of hills, with several summits (some marked by cairns and one other by the Ordnance Survey's triangulation point) is one of the most beautifully situated in all Wales and lies just about 50 miles from our starting point in Malvern Wells. The drive over into Radnorshire can be varied to one's choice but I find that going by the A44 (which runs from Worcester to Rhayader and then on to Aberystwyth) one can get to one's destination quicker than by the lesser roads which wind through the valleys and detain one with such glorious countryside! Fiona (my Golden Retriever) and I were anxious to make the most of the lovely day so we set off at 8·00am and were at our destination as the clock showed 9·30am and we did not have too much traffic with which to contend. Destination: this is important because there are many ways of walking Carneddau, as map 147 in the Landranger series will show but as we like the unusual we chose to turn off the A44 at Fforest Inn, where we picked up the A481 for Builth Wells and drove straight down it, passing 'Hundred House' and taking the small byroad opposite Matts Farm, signposted Howey and Llandrindod Wells; there are two such turns but be sure to take the later one on map reference 093538 (map 147) and almost at once turn *left* onto a *very* narrow road which leads right up into the hills passing farms on its way; glorious countryside: superb views and a road to drive with great care! The objective in this walk had been the trig. point on top of the Carneddau itself at 1,430 feet; also a cairn that can be found at 1,458 feet, a bit further on.

Objectives: the Trig Point at 1,430 ft. and the Cairn at 1, 456 ft.

Alas! neither were obtainable on this occasion because (as on the Brecon Beacons before) discretion had to be the better choice! We withdrew just as a blizzard swept in with great suddenness and so sent us off in a hurry by the way in which we had climbed. It remains something to he accomplished on another day.

The Carneddau – waiting until next time.

PART III

INTRODUCTION
TO THE LAST FEW PAGES
OF THESE ADVENTURES

In the years between 1989 and 1999 many things happened that made journeys and walking impractical, as well as impossible. In the first place my own health misfortunes held me homebound and recuperating. Secondly Fiona was getting older and although she lived to be 15½, and eventually died in my arms, she was active until the last week of her life but not for walking any distance. Then thirdly, we had the terrible scourge of *Foot and Mouth* disease which restricted both motorised journeys as well as any entry to farm land on the hills. So these final photographs and paragraphs are, after restrictions were lifted, journeys of observation to ensure 'all was still there'! That was prior to contemplating this book in 2008.

On the 16th June 1999 it dawned a fine day and at 5·00am treated the world awake at that time to a most glorious sunrise. Taking the old series OS Map 128 I set course for Wales – Powys in particular. At that time of the morning the roads were uncluttered and it was a pleasure to drive westwards towards the border where in and hour and ten minutes I was in Prestigne – some 46 miles. On then into the deeper heart of the Principality and some lovely single-track roads; first along B4356 to Llangallo and then on to Llanbisiter Road Station where those 'Early Birds' were awaiting a train on the single-track line to take them to work and to school. The road then climbs to high ground and at 8·27 am exactly and 61 miles on I crossed the cattle-grid onto moorland and I was in company with sheep as far as the eye could see! In the near and further distance were familiar hills that 'Fiona' and I had climbed: long ago (so it seemed!) but most wonderful of all was the total *silence:* a thing to be greatly treasured these days. The Buzzards, as usual, kept me company, and the day at that moment in time had to be called, serendipity...

It had not altered one tiny bit since my last visit in 1987: so after stretching my legs I followed my map with its arrows on the single-track road to 'Heartease'; this was a glorious route which only had a farm and cottages along its length. Continuing along this road for further miles one comes to what was my destination, Abbey Cwm Mir. This ancient ruin is well worth a visit but today it contained a story! Without my beloved Fiona I was alone, and to someone approaching from the valley below, to be encountered in passing. The setting among flowering rhododendrons of the adjacent Manor grounds was utterly peaceful and very beautiful. The Lady came up to pass me and she was crying: at the seat at that spot we both sat down and gradually encouraged, she poured out to me her unhappiness. She and her husband used to holiday here in a flat that was in the Manor House ... and he had just died: her visit was totally understandable. We talked; I listened a while; and then with gratitude for my comprehending and support she left to go her way homewards. The Church nearby, dedicated to St Mary seemed to call me over: afterwards I enjoyed a cup of coffee which a kind local body of people were organising at the end of that Church, especially for passing visitors. The Lady who served me asked wither I was bound, as I was leaving, and she directed me to Camlo Hill which I well remembered climbing with Fiona many years before and indeed my old map is marked atop with the margin-words 'Picnic spot with views!' – they were still there and I paused for a while and walked, and memories came back of a much longer walk but that was not now possible. It is still all a magical place which on this occasion had Mistle Thrushes, Yellowhammers, Bullfinches and above, several Buzzards, of course!

I lingered long enough to allow nature to send me on this occasion a Red Kite but today they were not to be seen, alas. So on over and down the hill and into Rhayader, but not onto the Elan Valley today. Turning left via a signpost marked *Howey* via Builth Wells and this back-road gives one lovely views of the Carneddau Hills where in the valley with this view one can (as I did) brew-up tea before setting off for home along the main road: to be home by 4·30pm and recorded 173 miles the round trip.

The Manor House adjacent to the Abbey of Cwm Mir.
The rhodadendrons can be seen on the right.

Abbey Cwm Mir ruins and trout pool.

A view of the Carneddau Hills outside Builth Wells, from the Howey Valley road.

DRUM DDU
(*1,554 ft.*)

8th July 1999

This time I set off at 6·15am with the Severn Valley in mist and the Malvern Hills with a haze on top, so it augured well for a fine day. Going via Ledbury and onto the Marcle road for Ross-on-Wye and then down the main road to the round-a-bout for Hereford but turning off that onto the road to Skenfrith (B4521). I stopped in the National Trust car-park for *Skirrid* (of earlier memories!) and photographed *Sugar Loaf* as well as *Skirrid* itself as it emerged from the haze; a very exciting sight so early in the morning. To this spot it was just 41 miles. Now it was down the road into Abergavenny and after finding the right road for *Brecon* I was off but on that main road, for a while. There was little traffic on it mercifully because after some 10 miles I ran into thick fog whereupon headlights became necessary and considerable caution. I arrived in *Brecon* at 8·15am after some 66 miles and parking in the main car-park I sought breakfast! The Wellington Hotel came to my rescue and after having a really excellent meal I was off again *in bright sunshine!!* Using my old OS Map 141 I found my way along a byroad onto the Mynydd Eppynt or as it is known today The Sennybridge Artillery Range. There was no red flag flying between 9·00 and 10·00am so I drove up to the very top and stopped at *The Drovers Arms* (now restored) and on to the romantic high point called

Drum Ddu at 1,554 feet. Superb views indeed so I could now see The Brecon Beacons: The Black Mountain (note singular!): the whole range of The Black Mountains: The Radnor Forest: The Begwns and The Carneddau. Unchanged panorama... Then driving over to the Observation Point, named *The Garth* I gazed at the fabulous vista of the valley below and the nearby highest mountain by the name of *Dygarn Fawr* at 2,115 feet. Certainly a place to refresh one's memories as to be sure that all one knew so well was still alive and beautiful. It would be hard indeed on such a day to improve on such experiences; and as it was by now getting very warm (82 degrees) a change of plan was called for: *Beulah* which my map showed as one, with almost an unbroken series of arrows either up or down, which was indeed a very, very pretty road with many spots to stop to walk, photograph and brew-up! After some more miles I turned off the road onto a track which headed into the hills and not finding any turning-place I came face-to-face with 'Evans the Post' going in the opposite direction! With that wonderful courtesy of the Welsh he backed a long way, into a gateway and we passed each other safely but not without an explanation as to why I appeared *'lost'!!* Back on the road for home it was then via the B4358 passing Gilwern Hill, Cregina and then *Llanbedr Hill* to stop to make my tea on top of course; then home to Leominster and Bromyard to record some 178 miles for the entire journey with many familiar hills and valleys seen on what was a beautiful summer's day.

Finally, on the 14th October 1999, during a period known to many as 'Indian Summer' or to others as 'St Luke's little summer' for his day in the Church calendar is October 18th: but whatever, it was a day for adventure into the hilltops of mid-Wales and weather-wise it was warm and gentle. I left home at 7·40am and travelling via the

A4103 to Hereford and round it on the ring-road to Sutton Sugwas and the A438 turning off at *Rhydspence* taking the byroad up the hill for Painscastle. This leads one onto the Begwns eventually but much map-reading may be necessary! This is an area much loved by Rally Enthusiasts of yesteryear and many's the time I've driven over it by night in a Mini-Cooper in a motor rally. I was for rediscovering some of this area's beauty and see the sheep and their shepherds again. By Map 141 of the old OS series there are many marks of mine indicating dangers, picnics and views – it is Powys, and it is truly beautiful. As I stopped for the first time it was 9·10am and some 45½ miles from home. I parked in a gateway out of the way and got out for a walk. Down into the valley I drove to *Painscastle* and then looked for a little tiny road to Lake Bwchllyn which IS still there and as peaceful as ever. On then up the hill – *Craig-Y-Fuddai* at 1,569 feet – to watch shepherds

The Garth viewpoint with a view of the valley.

gathering a large flock of sheep in the valley below. As I watched, a land-rover stopped in the gateway opposite and he got out. He came over to me and I learned his name was Glyn: he was a shepherd himself and he gave me half-an-hour's detailed revelation as to what and why they were doing what they were down in the valley below; a sort of explanatory 'One man and his dog' in real live scenario. Later he talked about himself; he then asked me why I was where I was? In telling him I also referred to my earlier fun in Rally Driving! "Oh!" he said "How we miss you all today"; I asked him why? "'Cos boy, in those days it was the only entertainment we had and as a boy to be up at 3 in the morning was rare fun!" So eventually we made ready to part, but sadly, not before he added quietly, "Now I must go and bury my dog".

Little was I to know then, that before another month was out I would be doing the same for Fiona. So this short chapter of my adventures seems to close quite naturally at this point, and I only have to add that as I headed for home, rather sadly after Glyn's news, I drove along main roads to Hereford and over Mordiford Bridge to Malvern registering exactly 100 miles and in time for tea at 3.30pm

Over the Begwm Hills – my 'road' home!
Wimple and Hergest ridge can be seen in the background.

AFTERWORD

The Author of these tales makes no claim to their total accuracy because other people travel at different speeds and take differing routes so that distances are not the same. The routes are by and large accurate to the various *tops* but it is wise to consult an up to date Ordnance Survey 1:50 000 (1.25 inch to 1 mile) to obtain detailed information. The Forestry Commission, for instance, introduces new roads which allow walkers; new parking places and also adds to their conifer plantations so that the map may not be totally accurate. In fine weather these walks and climbs are within the capabilities of the average walker and climber. Properly clad they should provide hours of joy on the hills within an hour or two's drive from Malvern and many are remote enough not to attract popular attention so a sense of exploration is heightened, and adventure coupled with discovery enhances the journey and the walk. To ensure that the 'Fionas' of this world are welcomed I make a plea for others who enjoy the remote hilltops to take extra care with their canine companions and if in any doubt ask the farmer or shepherd if a well behaved dog is allowed on the hillside. Similarly care should be taken to park one's car carefully so that no gateway or lane or trackway is obstructed for a larger vehicle (such as a tractor with trailer or Range Rover with horse box) and again if in doubt it is as well to ask permission before leaving a car for the day in a remote spot. In all our adventures Fiona and I found nothing but kindness and understanding; being able to speak a few words of Welsh made quite a difference with local farmers and shepherds who saw someone interested in their area and its natural life. Remember too that such local people know already that there are choughs or buzzards, peregrines or foxes, polecats or herons in the vicinity and they can often tell one better than any guide-book exactly what one has seen if one is in doubt!

MJS
Malvern
Worcestershire
August 2008

The author and Fiona 'On Top'!